THE ART
OF
MAKING WINE

THE ART OF MAKING WINE

BETTY SAMPSON

With illustrations by
ROSANNE SANDERS

AURUM PRESS

First published in hardback 1982 by Aurum Press Ltd,
10 Museum Street, London WC1A 1JS
Paperback edition published 1987
This revised edition published 1992

A catalogue record for this book is available
from the British Library

ISBN 1 85410 200 1

1 3 5 7 9 10 8 6 4 2
1993   1995   1996   1994   1992

Printed and bound in Great Britain by
The Bath Press, Avon

CONTENTS

FOREWORD

My first acquaintance with Betty Sampson was in the early seventies, when she was Secretary of the Kingsbridge Wine Circle. She was then already an established winemaker and later became an exhibitor of some distinction, subsequently qualifying as a wine judge.

In recent years, with the assistance of her husband and family, she has established an extensive new commercial vineyard in South Devon. With such a wealth of practical experience, it seems a natural progression for her to have written a book on winemaking.

All good wine has a certain balance. On reading the manuscript of this book it was immediately apparent to me that such a balance had also been achieved in putting the basic facts to beginners in simple terms, yet at the same time presenting enough technical content to satisfy the particular needs of established winemakers and exhibitors.

The recipe section is a masterpiece of application to the art of winemaking. Over a period of two years each recipe has been thoroughly tested to the author's own exacting standards before being included.

Betty Sampson brings to the following pages a breath of countryside, and blends it nicely with the science of winemaking. The result is unique. This superbly illustrated book is easy to understand, and will for many years meet the needs of new and old exponents of this absorbing pastime.

Peter K. Ineson
Convenor of Judges,
South West Counties Wine and Beermakers Federation

INTRODUCTION

Nostalgic memories from my childhood in the thirties include visits to my grandparents when occasionally my sister and I would be given a glass of a sweet, strong beverage poured from a bottle clearly labelled 'Elderberry Wine'. We sat in eager anticipation as the bottle was carefully brought out from under the stairs. The disapproving glances of our parents probably heightened our pleasure, but our greatest delight was the feeling of privilege in participating in these mysterious drinks to which Grandma coyly admitted she had added just a little tot of brandy.

Attitudes towards home winemaking have changed radically in recent years: the sweet, strong beverage of my grandmother's day would no longer be acceptable to our more sophisticated palates, and cheap travel and stronger ties with Europe have widened people's knowledge and removed some of the mystique for so long attached to the subject of wine. In those days home-made wines were normally drunk as a nightcap or for their warming effect before starting on a journey. Now they are usually consumed with a meal, so a much lighter, fresher wine is preferred. Techniques in home winemaking have changed beyond recognition, and a variety of winemaking utensils has been designed to meet the demands of the amateur. Increased knowledge of the process of fermentation and the prevention of bacterial damage by the careful use of chemicals have enabled winemakers to reach far higher standards of excellence than ever before.

My first venture into winemaking was in 1970 when my Devon garden produced an abundance of fruits which I could not utilise. Following this I helped in the formation of a local Wine Circle, of which I became an active member. The help and encouragement received from other members has been invaluable and I have enjoyed the challenge of entering competitions, both locally and at county and national level. Winning prizes is rewarding and provides the motivation towards greater achievements, but losing concentrates thoughtful attention to the problems and creates a desire to get things right. I have experienced both, and I am grateful to Show organisers who have given

me and other winemakers the opportunities of trying out our skills in competition. The general improvement in the quality of home-made wines can be partly attributed to this competitive spirit.

In most wine-producing countries the definition of wine is 'the product of the fermented juice of ripe grapes', but in cooler, more temperate climates this definition may be extended to include 'a similar liquor made from other fruits, juices, grains and flowers'. The grape is the perfect medium for winemaking in normal seasons as it contains the correct amount of sugars, acids, tannins, minerals and vitamins and this allows the yeast to ferment actively, converting the sugars to alcohol and carbon dioxide. In making country wines it is possible to come close to this special quality imparted by the grape. Acid, alcohol, aroma, body, flavour, texture and residual sugar all need to be balanced, whether the wine is dry, medium-dry or dessert. In order to obtain such a balance careful selection of ingredients is essential: the best wines are made when the sugars, acids and tannins in the fruit are at the correct levels and no additions or subtractions are required.

This perfect balance is the foundation stone of successful winemaking. Home winemakers often use only one type of fruit or vegetable, thereby giving to the wine the predominant character of that particular ingredient. Some will be high in acid or tannin and impart a strong flavour but will lack body and texture; to others the opposite will apply. A wine made from elderberries for example will contain a high proportion of flavour and tannin but will be lacking in acidity and body. Wines made primarily from bananas, pears or parsnips will have more body but will be lacking in interest and flavour owing to their low acidity. Many winemakers try to correct this imbalance by blending their wines together; my aim in the following recipes has been to achieve the correct balance at a much earlier stage—by the careful selection of ingredients that complement each other.

The recipes that I have devised for this book have all been tested and have consistently proved successful. They are divided into five sections: flower, fruit, vegetable, sparkling and dessert. The basic principles of winemaking are explained for the beginner, and there are sections devoted to fermentation, clearing, racking and some problems which may be encountered. Although I have attempted to keep all the instructions as straightforward as possible, the use of some technical terms is unavoidable. A simple explanation of these may be found in the Glossary on p. 125, and once the basic principles are understood the terms should present no problem.

The amateur winemaker's interest in commercial viticulture has been accelerated in recent years by visits abroad, when first-hand experience of tasting local wines has increased the desire to try a few vines in the garden. This enthusiasm prompted us to plant 60 vines in 1972 and eventually led to our establishing a four-acre vineyard in 1977 with 5,000 vines. Three more acres were planted in 1986 and in 1991 two more were added. Viticulture in Britain does not quite fulfil the idyllic picture brought home with our Mediterranean dreams but in good years a useful crop can be produced. I have devoted the last chapter to the production of grapes in the English garden.

I hope that this book will inspire those who have never made their own wine to begin; others who have never got beyond the first stages will perhaps be encouraged to experiment and develop their own recipes. Making wine is a fascinating hobby in itself—drinking it is the uniquely satisfying outcome.

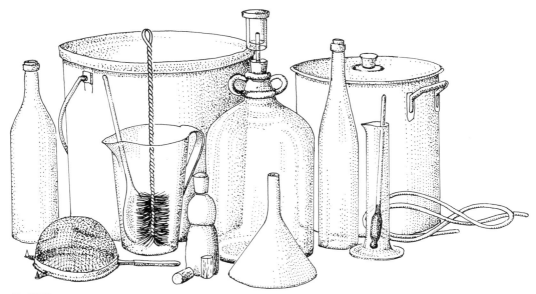

EQUIPMENT

Although some kitchen utensils may be used to start with, certain basic equipment will have to be purchased. This can be obtained from home-brew shops or departmental stores, and chemists now often carry a wide selection. A very simple 'Beginner's Kit' is given on p. 46, but for anyone at all serious about making wine, the following equipment will be needed.

Utensils
2 gallon plastic bucket with lid
Nylon sieve
Straining bags
Plastic funnel (6 inch, 15 cm, diameter)
Pyrex or plastic measuring jug
Large saucepan (preferably stainless steel)
Plastic syphon tubing (6 feet, 2 m)
Bottle brush
Fermentation bungs and airlocks
Two 1 gallon demijohns
Hand corker and corks
Hydrometer and jar
Long-handled wooden or plastic spoon
Bottles (these can often be obtained from friends or hotels)

Chemicals
Sodium metabisulphite or Campden tablets
Pectin-destroying enzyme (liquid or powder form)
Yeast nutrients (ammonium phosphate, ammonium sulphate, magnesium sulphate)

Vitamin B_1 tablets
Grape tannin or tannic acid (powder or liquid form)
Acid, preferably combined tartaric, malic and citric mixture

Utensils

The golden rule is never to use equipment made of any metal other than stainless steel. As this is expensive most items are made in white plastic, with the exception of saucepans. A few recipes advocate heating the ingredients using a stainless steel saucepan; if this type of pan is not available use a good quality saucepan and as soon as the required heat has been obtained remove the liquid to another container. The contents should never be allowed to stand in the vessel for any length of time. Wood is acceptable provided that it is kept scrupulously clean.

Plastic bucket with lid   It is essential for the plastic bucket or bin to have a tightly fitting lid. The size of the bucket will depend on the quantities you intend to make; if you are starting with very small quantities a gallon ice-cream container will suffice for a while.

Straining bags   As most of the ingredients will be infused in water for short periods or fermented on the pulp it is useful to have several straining bags. These may be purchased but the best and cheapest method is to make them yourself from remnants of nylon curtain material (select a firm net which has a fine mesh). The bags should be at least 16 × 14 inches (40 × 35 cm) for a two-gallon bucket and 20 × 17 inches (50 × 43 cm) for a five-gallon one.

It is a good idea, and essential for the larger sizes, to have two bags, one inside the other, to withstand the weight of pulp. This will also give a clearer juice as less pulp debris will escape into the receiving container. Do not make the bags with double net as small pieces of debris will become trapped between the layers, making it very difficult to clean them.

Airlocks   An airlock is necessary to exclude the air from the fermenting must while allowing the carbon dioxide to escape. The water level in the airlock should be about ½ inch (1.2 cm) and contain a little sulphite solution. Simple plastic ones are readily available which are fitted into the bored rubber bung.

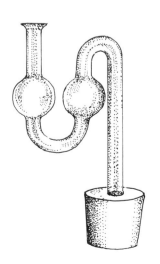 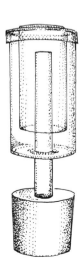 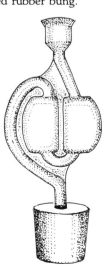

Demijohns   For most winemakers the glass demijohn is the best storage vessel as it is easy to handle and clean. Large glass containers are now more readily obtainable, and provided that enough storage space is available they are ideal for quantities of up to 6–8 gallons. Plastic containers are not suitable for long storage periods as they frequently impart a plastic taint to the wine. Small oak casks of 6–8 gallons are favoured by some winemakers, but they do need very careful attention to keep them free from stagnant or musty smells. Another problem which arises is the length of time the wine can be stored in them, as owing to the ratio of surface to the volume of wine premature and often excessive oxidation occurs.

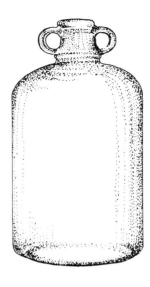

Hydrometer   Sooner or later the winemaker will have to become acquainted with a hydrometer. This is an instrument for measuring the specific gravity (S.G.) of a liquid compared with that of water, and although it may appear complicated it is in fact very simple to use. A hydrometer is invaluable in winemaking to estimate the quantity of sugar in the fruit juice so that calculations can then be made on the extra quantity of sugar needed to obtain the required alcoholic strength. The hydrometer can also be used as a guide to progress during fermentation and to ascertain when it is completed.

When making pure grape juice wines, wine from kits and other extracted fruit juices, or after straining the liquid from fruits infused in cold water or pasteurisation, an exact calculation can be made of the potential alcoholic strength of the finished wines by taking a hydrometer reading before adding the yeasts.

With fermentations on the pulp, however, hydrometer readings will give only a rough guide, as even if the reading is taken from some of the strained liquid before the yeast is added there will still be a considerable amount of sugar retained in the fruit pulp which will not be fully extracted until the yeast enzymes have finished their work.

Chemicals   Sodium or potassium metabisulphite (Campden tablets) have two important roles, one as a sterilising agent for equipment and the other to sterilise the prepared fruit ('must') and preserve the maturing wines.

Sulphite as a sterilising agent A solution of ½ oz (15 g) of sulphite crystals or 8 Campden tablets dissolved in 2 pints (1 litre) of warm water should be used for rinsing glassware and all other equipment before use. The solution can be kept in a tightly corked or screw-topped bottle for further use. A little may also be kept in demijohns that are not in use: if they are tightly corked they will remain bacteria-free until required. If containers are contaminated or dirty they should first be thoroughly cleaned with a chlorine-based steriliser before being rinsed two or three times with cold water, then with the sulphite solution and finally with cold water. It is a good policy to heat sterilise demijohns, airlocks, syphon tubes etc. twice yearly. Small plastic items should not be heated above 150°F (65°C).

Strong sulphite solution for must and wine Add 1 oz (30 g) sulphite crystals to ½ pint (284 ml) cold water, bottle and cork. Use according to recipe instructions.

Pectin-destroying enzyme   This can be purchased in powder or liquid form. It helps to facilitate pressing of fruit and increase the yield of juice, and

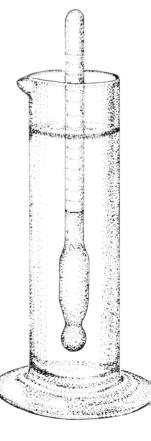

hydrometer in measuring jar

will also prevent a haze in the finished wine. Most brands give the quantity required for each gallon, usually one 5 ml teaspoonful per 4–5 lb of fruit. In cold water extractions you can add it in the initial stages of preparation, but if the ingredients are heated do not add until the liquid is at room temperature as the enzymes are destroyed by the heat.

Yeast nutrients   If the recipe does not include a high proportion of fruit or is made from flowers or vegetables it will require a nutrient for the development and growth of the yeast. Wines made with a high proportion of grapes or sultanas rarely need any additions. The main nutrients, ammonium phosphate, ammonium sulphate and magnesium sulphate, are usually sold under a proprietary brand name and contain all three chemicals.

Vitamin B_1 tablets   One tablet (3 mg) is usually sufficient for fruit and flower wines, but it is advisable to add two for wines made from vegetables or tinned fruits.

Acids and tannin   Most of the acids and tannin necessary will be obtained from the ingredients in the recipes, but a little extra will be required for flower and vegetable wines. Home winemaking stores sell packets of citric, malic or tartaric acids. The acidity may also be increased with lemon juice: 2 fl oz (56 ml) of lemon juice is equal to ¼ oz (7 g) of tartaric acid. Commercially prepared tannin can also be purchased but it is generally only required in vegetable or some flower wines.

BASIC PRINCIPLES AND INGREDIENTS

Methods of winemaking vary considerably from one person to another, and the individual style of each winemaker is reflected in the finished product. If you have developed a successful formula you should continue to use it, trying new experiments gradually and comparing the results. This chapter outlines the basic principles of winemaking; all the processes are described in greater detail in later chapters.

The recipes in this book are based on experiments which I have made over the past ten years. It was after I had spent a working holiday in the vineyards in the Rhinehessen that it became abundantly clear to me that the best wines are made only when all the essential ingredients have been extracted from the grapes. Quality wines are made from grapes with a high sugar content, with medium levels of tartaric and malic acids. In poor years an excessive amount of malic acid will still be discernible in the wine even after several years of maturing, and although the sugar content will have been adjusted it does not compare with the natural fruit sugars of the grapes. Bearing this in mind I started compiling recipes with the object of obtaining as much natural sugar and acid as possible from the fruits, selected to give a combination of acids, tannin and nutrients. As the grape is the perfect medium from which to get a vigorous and healthy fermentation plus good vinosity in the wine, the easiest and cheapest alternative must obviously be sultanas. They are of consistent quality with a very high sugar content, and their predominant acid is tartaric which is essential to balance the malic and citric acids of our home-grown fruits. In Germany and the Sauternes district of France the grapes that produce the sweet dessert wines are affected by the action of Botrytis cinerea, a fungus which attacks the grapes in warm humid conditions in late summer. This encourages a beneficial mould (*pourriture noble*) which extracts some of the liquid, leaving a sultana-type grape with a high concentration of sweet juice.

Most of the garden and country fruits used in winemaking have some natural sugars, but with high acid levels and pronounced flavours they need dilution with water in order to produce a drinkable wine within a reasonable maturing period. If sultanas are used to provide as much natural sugar and tartaric acid as possible, the level of garden or hedgerow fruits should not exceed more than two or three pounds per gallon (except in the case of apples and pears), otherwise the wine will contain an excessive amount of acid. As with grapes, the fruits will vary according to climatic conditions, and in very cold, wet summers it is advisable to reduce the garden fruits in proportion to the sultanas used; conversely, in particularly hot summers the acids will be lower and the sugar content higher, so extra garden fruits may be added. Good results may be achieved by replacing some of the sultanas with grape concentrate, and in the case of red wines more character will be achieved by including them. As most concentrates are balanced and contain sufficient acid for a gallon of wine the quantity added to a country wine should not exceed half a pint per gallon, except in making dessert wines when more acid is necessary.

In making sweet or dessert wines which need more flavour, acid and body, the predominant fruits should be increased, with the addition of bananas, sultanas, grape concentrate or pears. As these wines are more prone to bacterial infection the extra acid will help protect them. It also plays an important part during the maturing period in combining with alcohol to form esters, which contribute so much to the bouquet and aroma. With residual sugar present the acid is essential to give interest and zest to the wine.

During the process of fermentation the enzymes secreted by the yeast cells convert the sugars into ethyl alcohol and carbon dioxide. In order for the yeast to develop and multiply the enzymes require an adequate amount of nutrients in the form of ammonium phosphate and ammonium sulphate. Grapes contain sufficient nutrients for the yeasts, and recipes which combine a high proportion of grapes or sultanas with fresh fruits will rarely need any additions. Recipes based on dried, tinned or bottled fruits, however, benefit from the addition of a teaspoonful of yeast nutrient plus a Vit B_1 tablet. This applies also to flower and vegetable wines.

Different methods of fermentation

In order to obtain as much natural sugar, acids, tannin and nutrients from the fruit as possible, many of the recipes given here recommend fermentation 'on the pulp' *before* the addition of sugar. This reduces the time necessary for fermentation, thus reducing also the risk of bacterial infection and the formation of other unwanted substances which tend to get extracted by the alcohol as it is being produced. If no sugar has been added at this stage the enzymes concentrate their activity on the extraction and conversion of the natural sugars in the fruit and also on the tannins, acids and nutrients. In a vigorous fermentation most fruit sugars will be extracted within three days, but an extra day or two may be necessary for red fruit wines when a deep red colour is required with plenty of tannin.

In order to obtain the maximum amount of alcohol from a pulp fermentation, it is essential to keep the container or bucket tightly covered once the fermentation is really established. As the fermentation gets going the fruit pulp will be pushed to the top of the container by the force of the carbon dioxide gas, forming a cap. This must be broken up three or four times a day, to facilitate a quicker extraction rate.

In this type of fermentation a hydrometer is of limited value (see p. 14), so in order to estimate the amount of sugar present many books advise straining off enough liquid to test from the fruit pulp before fermentation takes place; this will give a rough guide to the extra sugar needed to obtain the desired alcoholic content. It does give a fairly accurate reading when you are using a grape concentrate, fresh grape juice, strained liquid after infusion in water or fruits with a low sugar content, but with fruits such as sultanas, raisins, dried apricots, figs and most of the pulpy fruits the sugars are only completely extracted after two or three days of pulp fermentation. As a rough guide one can estimate that just under half the weight of sultanas will be sugar.

The cold water extraction method is suitable for many soft fruits, with the addition of grape concentrate. The crushed fruits are placed in a sterile bucket with the recommended quantity of water, pectin enzyme, nutrients and sulphite (Campden tablets or sodium metabisulphite). They are then left for two days before being pressed. With this method a hydrometer reading can be taken which will give a reasonably accurate reading of the sugar present. The extra sugar required may be added in the form of a syrup, with the grape concentrate if used, once fermentation has begun. Juice extractors are suitable for many soft fruits, but not for the soft pulpy-fleshed fruits as these are often reduced to a puree.

Deep red fruits can be pasteurised: in this method the fruit is heated to a temperature of 150°F (65°C), kept at this temperature for five minutes and then allowed to cool gradually. Boiling fruits to extract the juice used to be the common practice, but this has lost favour in the past few years as it often imparts a 'cooked' flavour to the wine, which will lack the freshness of other methods.

Dried fruits such as apricots, peaches and prunes will make a cleaner wine if they are minced and treated under the cold water system. It is essential, however, that root vegetables should be boiled, and the liquid then strained off. If more than one or two bananas are used per gallon of wine, it is better to boil them for twenty minutes and strain off the liquid first, as otherwise the pulp tends to squeeze through the straining bag.

The ingredients

It cannot be said that any one constituent of wine takes priority over another; they all have an essential part to play, and the winemaker's art lies in balancing these constituents to their best advantage.

Fruits and flowers

In selecting ingredients always remember that the quality of your wines will depend on the quality of the ingredients. Fruits should be fully ripe, and any mouldy ones must be discarded. Vegetables should be scrubbed thoroughly and flowers picked on a fine day and processed quickly. Frozen fruits can be used successfully for winemaking, and even fruits whose cell walls collapse when thawed are ideal as this makes juice extraction easier. One of the advantages of freezing is that it helps to reduce costs, since fruit may be bought in the summer months when it is plentiful and kept to be augmented by other cheaper fruits in the autumn and winter.

Some country fruits may be difficult to obtain. Bilberries, for example, grow in profusion in some moorland areas but are almost unobtainable elsewhere.

These can be purchased frozen, dried or bottled (the imported Polish ones are excellent) and a small quantity will impart a pleasant flavour to the wine. Sloes and bullaces may also be difficult to find, and if they are you can substitute half damsons and half blackcurrants. Elderberries and blackberries are generally plentiful in the hedgerows, and fruits such as gooseberries, blackberries, redcurrants, cherries, raspberries, loganberries, damsons, plums, apples and pears very rarely fail in the garden, and can always be purchased quite readily in season. Fruits from warmer climates such as apricots, peaches and grapes are now available in the shops over quite a long period.

When choosing ingredients for home-made wines it is far better to use a blend of fruits rather than a single one. Some fruits naturally complement each other, while others do not harmonise. A bland fruit needs something to give interest and life to the wine. Apples and pears are good supplements to fruits such as apricots, peaches, pineapples and most of the red fruits. Strawberries on their own tend to produce a rather insipid wine with an overpowering bouquet, but adding a small quantity of blackcurrants will turn it into a very pleasant rosé. It is far better to blend fruits during the initial stages when they have a chance to harmonise, rather than blending the wine at a later stage.

Flower wines receive much criticism, largely because the flowers' contribution is in the form of bouquet and aroma with very little vinosity. These wines should be light and early maturing. In order to balance the bouquet some type of fruit which will not detract from the delicacy of the wine should be used. The recipes for flower wines in this book are mainly based on the use of sultanas, preferably the white Australian ones which will not impart too much flavour. Some garden fruits can be used, but only in a limited quantity otherwise the acid content will be too great.

Vegetable wines take a long time to mature, so many winemakers today cannot be bothered with them. Root vegetables need supplementing with fruit in order to give the wine character; their acid and sugar content is minimal but they do contribute body and flavour. Green vegetables such as pea pods and nettles supply some of the nitrogenous matter necessary for fermentation, and quite successful wines can be made from these and from vine prunings and oak leaves, but unless they are supplemented with grape concentrate or sultanas they often prove thin and lacking in character.

As already emphasised, the quality of the fruits used is of paramount importance in imparting their full flavour to the finished wine. They also provide a source for the trace elements, which are of such vital importance. A chemical analysis reveals that the average composition of wine is 85 per cent water, 14.5 per cent acids, glycerol, alcohol, tannin and sugars, and the remaining 0.5 per cent the vital volatile and fixed constituents which transform it from the 'vin ordinaire' into the 'classic' class.

Acid

Acid is necessary to achieve a strong healthy fermentation, and it contributes greatly to the wine's flavour and character as well as helping to protect the wine from bacterial infections and acting as an anti-oxidising agent. Without sufficient acid the wine would taste bland and medicinal.

The three main acids, tartaric, malic and citric, each play a different role and the recipes given here are formulated to include fruits with some of each. As you become more experienced you may wish to be able to control the acidity of your wine to a greater degree of accuracy. Acid testing kits may be obtained from most home-brew shops, and these give instructions on procedure and recommend the quantities of acid required for each type of wine.

Tannin

Tannin is found significantly in the skins of fruits, with red fruits containing a higher proportion than whites. Fruits that have a high tannin concentration are elderberries, bilberries, sloes, damsons, grapes, including dried grapes (i.e. sultanas and raisins), pears and gooseberries.

One of the chief functions of tannin is to give astringency to the wine. This is particularly important for deep red wines which rely on tannin to provide vigour and depth. It is also a major factor in conservation and clarification, as it combines with proteins and allied nitrogenous substances which otherwise tend to give hazes in later stages. Because of their high tannin content red wines taste very harsh when they are first made and take longer to mature.

Nutrients

Additional nutrients are sometimes necessary to 'feed' the yeast and maintain a vigorous fermentation. Most proprietary brands of yeast nutrient contain ammonium phosphate, ammonium sulphate and magnesium sulphate. Some contain only the former two ingredients, and if you live in a soft water area a pinch of Epsom salts will replace the magnesium sulphate. One or two Vit B_1 tablets are essential for vegetable and flower wines, but well-balanced fruit recipes with the right proportion of grapes or sultanas will ferment adequately with the nutrients extracted from the fruits.

Pectin

Most fruits contain pectin, which is essential in making jams and jellies; in winemaking it is not desirable, however, as it sometimes leaves an opaque haze in the wine. To overcome this problem pectin-destroying enzymes are used, which decompose the pectic substances in the early stages. Pectin-destroying enzymes are easily obtainable under a number of trade names, and a small quantity is recommended in the recipes given here.

Sugar

In making wine the main aim is to obtain all the sugars that are in the fruits, but however much attention is devoted to extracting as much natural sugar as possible from the ingredients it will still be necessary to add sugar in order to obtain the required amount of alcohol. The cheapest and most suitable form to use is ordinary white granulated cane or beet sugar. It is best to make this into a syrup, which will mix more easily with the strained liquid (the 'must').

Yeast

No wine can be produced without the aid of yeasts. Their purpose is to break down organic substances by means of the enzymes which they secrete; in winemaking it is necessary for the sugars to be broken down into alcohol and carbon dioxide.

There are many types of yeasts, some beneficial in winemaking and others termed 'wild'. Yeasts exist on all fruits, and can be seen on the skins of some fruits (known as the bloom).

Both good and wild yeasts will reach the fermentation jars when you are making wine. The wild yeasts will multiply if they have access to oxygen, but if a small amount of sulphite is added to the prepared fruit the sulphur dioxide released will displace the oxygen, so inhibiting their growth. The wine yeasts can more easily withstand sulphite, and as they are anaerobic (that is, they can develop without oxygen) they will soon build up an active colony and rapidly gain control. Furthermore they are protected by the build-up of carbon dioxide and increasing alcohol content which the wild yeasts are unable to tolerate. For this reason it is essential not to expose the fruit pulp for any length of time once fermentation has begun.

Various wine yeasts are in plentiful supply in most winemaking shops. Do not use brewer's or baker's yeasts, as these may impart a yeasty flavour to the wine and they generally have a poorer alcohol tolerance. Wine yeasts are available in cultured or dried form. The cultured yeasts are expensive but are more true to type and worth while if you intend to make several batches. The next most desirable are in sealed tablet form. They can also be purchased in tubs or jars, but the risk of infection is then greater although many winemakers appear to use them without any problems. It is advisable to use a type of yeast as near as possible to the character of wine you intend to make: Burgundy or Bordeaux for table reds, Hock or Chablis for the light whites, Sauternes for sweeter whites and Tokay for dessert reds.

reaction of yeast in demijo

Yeasts require an acidic solution with nutrients and vitamins in order to multiply and create an active fermentation. In wines containing a high proportion of fresh fruits these elements will be extracted by pulp fermentation; but if fruits are infused in water or pasteurised before pressing some extra nutrient may be necessary. If only a small quantity of fruit is used or the main ingredients are vegetables or flowers these essential additives must be included to ensure a healthy fermentation.

Yeasts are inhibited if too high a ratio of sugar to water is added before a vigorous colony has been formed. This is a trap that many beginners fall into: too much sugar syrup is added initially to the strained must, resulting in an over-concentrated solution which kills off the yeast. What happens, in simple terms, is that water in the fermenting yeast cells is transferred through the yeast cell walls to dilute the highly concentrated sugar solution; if this process of osmosis is too extreme the cells—which are 50 per cent water—become dehydrated and eventually die.

Glycerine
Glycerine is a product of fermentation and the quantity present in wine is quite high, sweet wines usually having twice the amount of the drier types. It creates a softness and roundness which is of great importance in the finished wines.

Water
Country wines rely on the use of water, and several pints are included in each gallon of wine. If you have a clean water supply there is no need to boil the water before use, but if in doubt or if it contains a taint of chlorine boil it first and cool before use.

Sulphite

The purifying qualities of sulphur have long been known to winemakers, and even today in some European wineries sulphur candles are still burned inside the wooden casks to kill bacterial organisms. Sodium metabisulphite and potassium metabisulphite are available in crystalline powder form, or you can buy them in proprietary form as Campden tablets.

Sulphite is used primarily for sterilising equipment and stabilising the finished wine, but a small quantity is also used in the preparation of the must to inhibit wild yeasts and kill bacteria, which are very sensitive to its presence. For sweet wines the quantity used will be slightly greater and this will also help to promote the glycerine formation during fermentation. When the wine is maturing sulphite helps to safeguard it against bacterial infection, assists clarification and stabilisation and acts as an anti-oxidant.

In wines containing a high quantity of fruit much of the sulphite is used up in combining with sugars, aldehydes and acids to form bisulphite compounds, so the amount of sulphur dioxide left to protect the wine against bacterial infection is greatly reduced. It is very important to remember that these fuller, sweeter wines will need extra sulphite when fermentation is completed.

PREPARATION OF THE MUST AND CONTROL OF FERMENTATION

The dictionary definition of must is 'unfermented or only partially fermented juice'. It is only when the fermentation is complete that the must becomes wine.

The must is a combination of ingredients from which the wine will be made, and its quality and character will depend to a large extent on the choice and preparation of ingredients at this critical stage. The way the ingredients are processed will enhance or damage the final quality of the wine: the ripeness and condition of the fruits or the amount of sunshine on the flowers are important factors.

Provided that the ingredients are in good condition, the method of preparation and control of fermentation play the next most important parts. The choice of preparation falls into four categories:

1 *pulp fermentation:* the extraction of sugar, acids,
    nutrients, etc. by the yeast enzymes;
2 *cold water infusion:* steeping the ingredients in water
    before adding the yeasts;
3 *pasteurisation:* extraction by heat;
4 *juice extraction:* by force or pressure.

All will give satisfactory results, but the finished wines will have different characteristics according to the method used. These are described in detail on pp. 25–32.

The right temperature

The control of temperature also plays a crucial part in the retention of bouquet and flavour. In fermenting small quantities of wine it is essential to keep the jars at temperatures of 60°F (16°C) for white wines, although strains of yeast have been developed which will ferment at temperatures as low as 50°F (10°C). Red wines need a slightly higher temperature of 65°F (18°C). During the vigorous primary fermentation these lower temperatures are adequate, but as it nears completion the fermentation will slow down and may be moved to a warmer place. When larger quantities are fermented heat is retained within the bulk of the wine and so fermentation will take place satisfactorily in cooler surroundings. (In Germany and California it is common practice to ferment commercially at low temperatures with the result that the wine produced retains more bouquet and flavour.)

Activating the yeast

Many wine yeasts will activate by adding them directly to the bulk, but as it is important for the fermentation to start quickly, to alleviate the risk of bacterial problems, it is advisable to activate the specialised tablet yeasts or yeast cultures 24 hours in advance, so that a sizeable colony is established before adding to the bulk. A suitable starter medium can be prepared as follows.

Yeast starter

Dissolve 1 dessertspoon sugar in ¼ pint (142 ml) warm water, add the juice from ½ lemon (approx. 25 ml) and a small pinch of yeast nutrient and the yeast culture. Pour into a sterilised bottle; the solution should three-quarters fill the bottle. Plug the top with cotton wool and stand in a warm place (65–70°F, 21°C) for 24 hours.

When adding the active yeast starter to the must it is a good idea to leave a small amount in the bottom of the bottle and top it up with a little more starter medium, in case the development of the colony is retarded by the level of sulphite still remaining in the must. If this happens the remaining yeast starter can be added in 24 hours, or if not needed it can be used for the next batch. It should be stored in the refrigerator, but do not keep it for longer than a week as the risk of bacterial infection is always present.

Methods of extraction

1 Pulp fermentation

All equipment must be thoroughly cleaned. It should be rinsed with a sulphite solution and then rinsed again with cold water. All fruits must be free from moulds. Hard fruits can be washed, sultanas should be washed and minced or lightly liquidised, soft fruits crushed or liquidised. Flower petals should be

starter bottle plugged with cotton wool

UPTURNED PLATE

FRUIT CAP

FERMENTING MUST

carefully checked for foreign bodies and all the green calyx should be removed or it will impart a bitter flavour. Do not wash petals. Remove as many stones as possible from apricots, plums, cherries, bullaces, sloes, etc. (care should be taken not to crack the stones as this too will give an unpleasant flavour).

Add the recommended quantity of cold water, pectin enzyme, sulphite solution or Campden tablets, yeast nutrient and Vit B_1 tablets. Stir well and cover. Leave for 24 hours before adding the active yeast starter, which should be carefully poured into the top of the must. Do not stir into the bulk at this stage, but wait for about 12 hours until an active colony has developed before stirring it in. In order to extract the maximum sugar and acid from the fruits it is essential to keep the fruit cap submerged as far as possible. The cap should be broken up several times each day, and this can be done most easily with an upturned plate kept on top of the must.

The bucket must always be kept tightly covered. If the cover does not fit well place a sheet of polythene sheeting over the top and secure with a strong elastic band before putting on the cover. This will also be effective in the case of larger bins.

If the fermentation is really active two days is usually adequate to extract all the sugars and acids from the pulp, but a red wine may require an extra day or two to get a deep red colour and extra tannin for its development. After the pulp has fermented for the period recommended in the recipe, place the sterile straining bag into another container of similar size and pour in the fermenting must. Lift the edges of the bag and agitate it slowly from side to side so that most of the liquid drains through. Pour this into the gallon demijohn and fit an airlock. Twist the top of the straining bag lightly and after washing the original bucket free of any remaining fruit pulp place the 'pudding' of the pulp on an upturned glass dish in the bucket. Replace the lid immediately and leave for 12 hours, when the remaining must will have drained free. (If you are making a larger quantity in a bin, use an upturned plastic bucket to support the straining bag.) This method helps to reduce the risk of bacterial infection, as the fermenting pulp and must still continue to build up carbon dioxide, thus protecting the wine during the straining period.

**pour must through sterile
straining bag**

twist the top of the bag

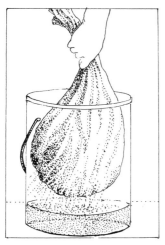

lift bag to allow must to drain

**place bag on upturned bowl
to drain further**

Pour the remaining strained must into the fermenting jar and add the sugar syrup (see below). The jar should be only seven-eighths full, to allow for any excessive frothing which may occur. After a few days top up to the neck of the jar with cold boiled water.

Sugar solution
*Dissolve 1 lb of sugar to ½ pint of water (approx. 500 g to 300 ml) over
a slow heat. Extra quantities should be made in the same proportions.*

strained must

seven-eighths full after addition of sugar

airlock fitted

topped up after a few days

2 Cold water infusion

The crushed ingredients plus the pectic enzyme, nutrients, Vit B_1 tablet and teaspoonful of strong sulphite solution (see below) or Campden tablet are placed in the plastic bucket and infused in the recommended quantity of cold water for two or three days. Since the extraction rate will not be as great as in pulp fermentation, this method is more suitable for soft fruits which can be easily crushed, thus releasing the juice more readily. The acid and tannin content will also be less with this method than with pulp fermentation, resulting in an earlier-maturing wine.

As there will be a certain amount of sugar and acid left in the pulp some winemakers use this pulp again with a little extra fruit for a pulp fermentation to make another gallon of wine. The success of these 'second' wines is of course dependent on the first extraction rate: if the vital ingredients have been extracted satisfactorily the remaining pulp will have only a minimal and unknown value.

When using the cold water infusion method it is possible to obtain a fairly accurate record of the amount of sugar contained in the must by using a

---

Strong sulphite solution for must and wine
Add 1 oz of sodium or potassium metabisulphite to ½ pint of water (approx. 30 g to 300 ml). Store in a screw-topped bottle.

---

hydrometer. This is an instrument which indicates the specific gravity or density of a liquid being measured compared with the density of water. In a heavy syrupy solution the hydrometer will float high, giving a high reading, whereas in water or after fermentation is completed it floats just off the bottom of the measuring jar with a low reading.

The starting specific gravity (S.G.) of the must should not exceed 1.090 after the sugar is added. This is adequate for light white table wines, but a little more sugar will be required for the heavier red wines. The extra sugar should be added later, after the fermentation is under way. All sweet and dessert type wines will need additional sugar.

After you have strained the must from the pulp, check the temperature. It should be 60°F (16°C); if above or below this level a correct reading will not be achieved.

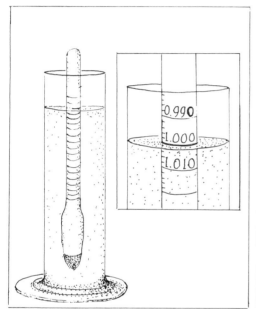

hydrometer in water

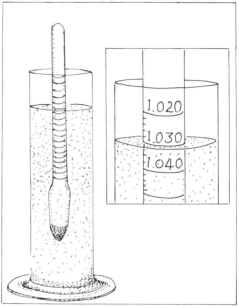

strained must

Pour some of the strained must into a measuring jar and take the reading. If the specific gravity is below 1.090 it will be necessary to bring it up by adding sugar. Each extra pound of sugar per gallon will raise the density by 35, so if for example the reading is 1.030, you will need to add 26 oz sugar in the form of sugar syrup to reach the optimum requirement.

Pour the must into a demijohn and add the yeast starter. The demijohn should not be more than seven-eighths full to allow for the possibility of excessive frothing. Plug the jar with cotton wool and leave in a warm place (65°F, 18°C). When the fermentation is active remove the cotton wool and fit an airlock.

After a few days it will be necessary to top up to the neck of the jar with a weak sugar syrup (½ lb to 1 pint of water) in order to keep the strength of the must constant.

As the fermentation nears completion the specific gravity will drop to between 990 and 1.000. If a dry wine is required the S.G. reading should be nearer the lower figure. Many winemakers like there to be some residual sugar, however; this can be achieved either by sweetening the wine before bottling, when all the yeast cells have been eliminated, or by racking (see p. 33) when the S.G. reaches 996 and removing to a cool place.

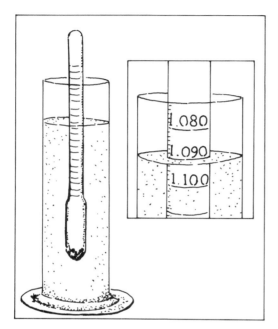

after adding sugar

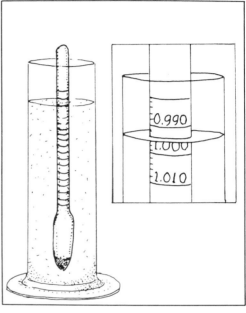

fermentation completed

3 Pasteurisation

A good extraction rate can be achieved when making red wines by heating or pasteurising the ingredients for a controlled period. This will extract more colour and flavour without including a high proportion of acids and tannin, which is inevitable with some red fruits if fermented on the pulp. The wine will be lighter in texture and will mature more quickly, but it will lack some of the character of the deep red wines. Fruits particularly suitable for this method are elderberries, sloes, bullaces, blackcurrants, damsons, bilberries and blackberries.

Pasteurisation prevents bacterial spoilage and eliminates the necessity to add sulphite to the must in the preparation state. As the ingredients are not boiled the wine retains a clean, fresh flavour which is destroyed with boiling.

The ingredients should be washed, liquidised or chopped. Add the required amount of cold water and heat to 150°F (65°C), maintaining this temperature for five minutes. Remove from the heat and leave to cool. If you do not have a culinary thermometer, bring the required amount of water to the boil, add all the ingredients and leave over a very low heat for five minutes, stirring all the time. When cool pour the mixture into a covered bucket, adding the pectic enzyme, Vit B_1 tablet and yeast nutrient. Leave for 24 hours, then strain and take the hydrometer reading to assess the sugar present in the must. Calculate the amount of sugar necessary to bring the specific gravity up to 1.090 (see p. 124), but do not add the sugar at this stage. Pour into a demijohn with the yeast starter and plug with cotton wool. The fermentation should be active within 24 hours, when sugar in the form of sugar syrup may be added.

4 Juice extraction

Centrifugal juice extractors have a limited use and are suitable for some fruits, for example apples, oranges, raspberries, loganberries and blackberries. Care should be taken with citrus fruits to exclude the peel which will impart a bitter taste to the wine. Most fruits are strongly flavoured and have a high acid content so they will need to be diluted with water.

After you have measured the specific gravity and calculated the amount of sugar needed, pour the liquid into a demijohn with the pectin enzyme, nutrients and yeast starter. Once the fermentation is active the sugar may be added in the form of syrup (see p. 27).

If you have a really large quantity of grapes to process it may be necessary to buy a fruit press, but quite sizeable amounts can be managed satisfactorily

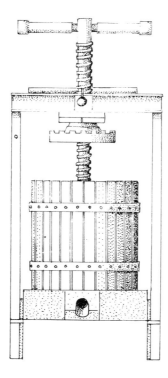

using a household liquidiser. Take care to liquidise them for a few seconds only – long enough to break the skins but not to damage the seeds, or too much tannin will be released. Leave the crushed grapes in a covered bin or bucket overnight with 1 crushed Campden tablet or 1 teaspoon (5 ml) of strong sulphite solution and 2 teaspoons of pectin enzyme per 15 lb (7 k) of grapes. This will facilitate the pressing and give a better yield of juice.

Whatever the extraction method chosen, as soon as the must is poured into the fermentation jars it will follow a similar pattern. During the first few days fermentation will be very vigorous, and this will be apparent from the speed of the popping airlock releasing the carbon dioxide. After several days the rhythm becomes slower as the available sugar decreases, and fermentation will finally cease. In table wines this process should be completed in two or three weeks, when the specific gravity should have dropped to below 1.000.

Social and dessert wines need to have a higher alcoholic content, which is achieved by adding more sugar syrup. In making these wines, sugar syrup must be added as soon as the hydrometer reading drops to a specific gravity of 1.005, bringing it up to 1.015 again. For social wines this process should be repeated once more. In order to achieve the higher alcoholic content for dessert wines, additions of sugar syrup should be added each time the S.G. drops to 1.005 until fermentation finally ceases. Up to six or seven additions may be necessary before the level of alcohol finally kills the yeasts. As a rough guide, the S.G. of social wines should be in the region of 1.005 to 1.010, and the fruity, full-bodied dessert wines from 1.015 to 1.030.

When the fermentation has finished remove the jar to a cool place and rack according to the instructions in the following chapter.

MATURING: RACKING, CLEARING AND BOTTLING

Racking

The heavy deposit, known as lees, which forms on the bottom of the jar as fermentation proceeds is mainly composed of yeast debris and insoluble salts. If these dead yeast cells and debris are left for too long they begin to decompose, with the consequent production of 'off' flavours. It is of paramount importance, therefore, as soon as fermentation is completed, to syphon off the clearing wine from the lees (see illustration, p. 34). Top up to the neck of the jar with a little cold water; this is essential to prevent oxidation. Replace the airlock and remove to a cooler place. After two days syphon again into a clean jar, adding 2 crushed Campden tablets or 2 teaspoons (10 ml) of strong sulphite solution. Top up again with cold water, but this time replace the airlock with a cork bung. This quantity of sulphite will inhibit most remaining yeast cells and give a high protection against bacterial problems.

The wine will need racking again after three weeks, with the addition of another crushed Campden tablet or 1 teaspoon (5 ml) of strong sulphite solution.

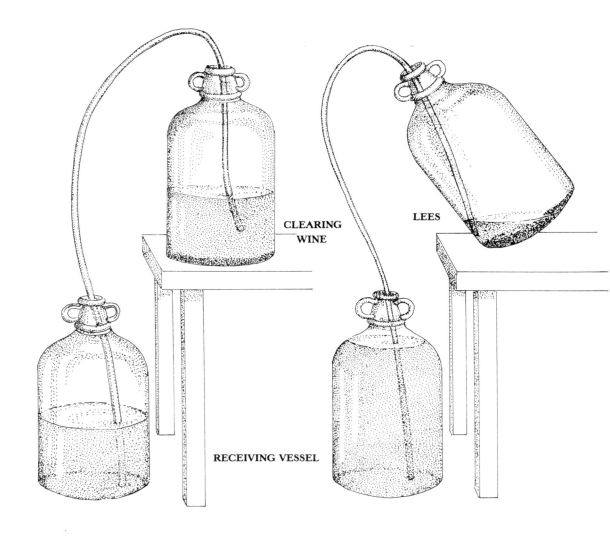

CLEARING WINE

LEES

RECEIVING VESSEL

It is important not to aerate the wine too much during the racking process. as this will reduce the proportion of sulphur dioxide remaining in the wine. The syphon tube should be placed at the bottom of the receiving vessel to prevent aeration.

Place the jar on a table or draining board carefully so as not to disturb the sediment. Put an empty sterile jar below on the floor. Take the syphon tube, which should be about 6 foot (2 metres) long, and place the tube in the jar above the sediment, taking care not to disturb it. Suck the wine gently up the tube, and when it is full quickly put your index finger over the end of the tube and lower it into the bottom of the receiving jar. The wine will flow freely as long as the end of the tube in the upper jar is submerged. As the upper jar empties gently tilt it to remove as much liquid as possible without disturbing the sediment. Top up with cold water and replace the bung.

Clearing

The wine should be stored in a cool dark place to mature. This is not always possible in modern houses, but try to select a place where the temperature does not vary too greatly. It is better to store it in a constant temperature of 60°F (16°C) than in one which changes rapidly with weather conditions. Some wines will clear quite quickly but others need a longer maturing period. As soon as a deposit forms which covers the bottom of the jar you should rack again. It is very important at this stage to avoid oxidising the wine, so make certain that the syphon tube is always kept at the bottom of the receiving vessel.

The recipes recommend a large dose of sulphite after the second racking and a smaller dose on the third racking in order to prevent bacterial or secondary fermentation which will cause a haze. Except for an infected wine these are the only doses the wine should receive. Most red wines will clear fairly quickly on account of their high tannin content. The negatively charged tannins are attracted to the positively charged proteins in suspension to form insoluble groups which by their weight precipitate or settle to the bottom. White wines which also have proteins in suspension do not however contain so much tannin, especially if they are not fermented on the pulp.

An alternative way of neutralising these positive protein particles is to use a small quantity of Bentonite, which has a negative charge. This should be made up in solution (see below) and added to the wine. Care must be taken not to add too much otherwise instead of a positive haze composed of the protein a negative haze caused by the Bentonite will result. The quantity of Bentonite should not exceed 1 g per gallon. Once added it should be allowed to settle for

---

Bentonite
Put about 4 fl oz (120 ml) water in a small bottle and add 1 g Bentonite. Shake well and leave for an hour before shaking again. Repeat until Bentonite has dissolved.

---

a week, and if this fails to clear the wine a gelatine and tannin fining can be added six hours before adding another gram of Bentonite. (As a guide use ½ g gelatine and ¼ g tannin per gallon.)

It is impossible to say exactly how long the wine will take to clear. Wines are made from natural products and these will vary from season to season according to the climatic conditions. If in doubt it is far better to rack the wine once more and wait a little longer for it to mature.

Filtering

To obtain a 'star bright' quality it will be necessary to filter the wine, using cellulose filters. Inexpensive filter kits can be bought for small quantities of wine, or if you are making several gallons you can use the large hand pump filters. Both are very effective. To prevent a filter taint you should flush the filter through with water for 15 minutes, followed by a small quantity of wine which should then be discarded.

Filtering gives a final polish to the wine. Do not attempt to remove a heavy sediment or haze in this way, however, for it will just clog the filter.

Bottling

Throughout the making of the wine great care has been taken to ensure that it is free from microbial organisms. It is important during the final stage that every effort is made to maintain this standard so that the wine will keep and improve in bottle; carelessness or indifference at this time could ruin the efforts that have gone into the earlier stages. If careful racking has been carried out dry red and white table wines should have adequate free sulphur dioxide remaining in them to give protection during their bottled life, but if the wines are going to be sweetened extra protection will be necessary against bacterial and secondary fermentation. Many winemakers prefer to take the edge off the dryness by adding 1 oz (30 g) of sugar per gallon at this stage, but if more than this quantity is used it is advisable to add 2 crushed Campden tablets or 2 teaspoons of strong sulphite solution before bottling.

When selecting bottles make sure they are in keeping with the type of wine produced. A deep red wine is traditionally bottled in a green Bordeaux or Burgundy type bottle. Not only does this add to the anticipation as the wine is poured but the quality of the wine is maintained, for strong light will adversely affect both the colour and the quality of red wines. White or rosé wines can be bottled in Hock bottles, or if they are kept in a dark place in white Bordeaux or tinted Burgundy bottles.

If the bottles you are using are not new they should be thoroughly cleaned with a chlorine steriliser and then rinsed two or three times in cold water. Rinse them finally with a mild sulphite solution (1 Campden tablet to 2 pints of water) and drain in a sterile bucket for twenty minutes before use. New bottles should be rinsed with sulphite solution and drained in the same way.

Care should be taken to obtain good quality corks, which must be smooth and even-grained. Before bottling soak them for two hours in a mild sulphite solution; do not use boiling water or the corks will lose some of their elasticity and become hard. As the corks will tend to float to the surface a weighted container should be placed over them to keep them submerged.

The wine may now be syphoned from the jar into the clean bottles, following the same procedure as racking by placing the bottles at a lower level so that the wine flows freely. When the bottle is nearly full place your index finger over the end of the tube and transfer it to another bottle. Bottles should be filled to within about 2½ inches (6 cm) of the top, allowing an air space of ¾ inch (2 cm) between the wine and the cork.

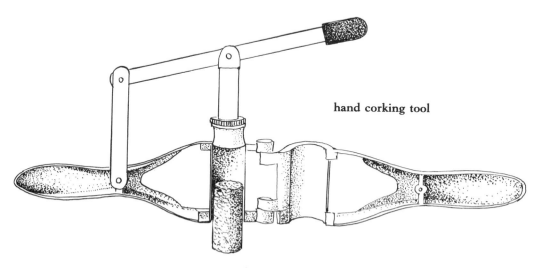

hand corking tool

A hand corking tool may be used to drive the cork home flush with the top of the bottle, and a plastic or foil capsule can then be fitted over the cork. The wine should be clearly labelled with details of the variety, type and date of production; attractive labels can be found in winemaking shops and will add to the appearance of your wine.

The wine should be stored on its side to prevent the cork from drying out; if this happens the cork may shrink, with the possibility of air and spoilage organisms reaching the wine.

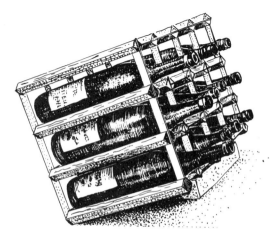

SOME POTENTIAL PROBLEMS

If the basic rules of winemaking are followed with reasonable care very few difficulties should arise, but occasionally, since we are all human, failures will occur. Some may be capable of remedy, others not; but knowing the reasons for them may prevent you making the same mistakes again. It is important to keep detailed records of the ingredients used and the method of juice extraction and fermentation so that as wines reach maturity you can assess and compare their merits and defects.

Stuck fermentation

One of the most common faults, especially among beginners, is a 'stuck' fermentation. This means that fermentation has ceased before all the sugar has been fermented by the yeasts, leaving an excessively sweet wine. There are several different causes of a stuck fermentation, and it is best to check first for faults which are the easiest to remedy.

1 Temperature   This should be in the region of 60–65°F (16–20°C). If the temperature has dropped to 50°F (10°C) or less there is a possibility that the yeast cells have become dormant, so the must should be moved to a warmer place when they will gradually become more active. If on the other hand the wine has been kept in a temperature of 80–85°F (27–29°C) this heat will have killed the yeast cells and the must will have to be restarted (see 5, below).

2 Nutrients   Check that you added nutrients and Vit B_1. If the must has a low fruit content or vegetable and flower wines are being made it is essential to add 1 teaspoon (5 g) of nutrients and 1 Vit B_1 tablet.

3 Acid   Yeasts ferment more actively in an acid medium, so check whether the must lacks acid. If it tastes insipid add 2 fl oz (56 ml) of lemon juice.

WINE RECORD SHEET

TYPE _DAMSON_ DATE _10.2.81_

INGREDIENTS _3lb damsons : 1 teasp. pectin enzyme_

½lb bananas : 1 teasp. yeast extract

4 pints water : 1 Vit B₁ tab : Burgundy
type yeast

TYPE OF
FERMENTATION _Pulp_

DATE STRAINED _13.2.81_ S.G. READING _1.000_

ADDITIVES _½ lb sugar_

¾ pint red grape
concentrate

S.G. READING _1.064_

FERMENTATION
COMPLETED _24.2.81_ S.G. READING _992_

1st RACKING _24.2.81_

2nd RACKING _25.2.81_ ADDITIVES _2 crushed_
Campden tablets

3rd RACKING _30.3.81_ ADDITIVES _1 crushed_
Campden tablet

COMMENTS _Wine_
clearing quickly with heavy deposit

4th RACKING _28.7.81_ COMMENTS _Clear,_
good bouquet, still harsh
30.11.81 Clean and fresh, ready to
bottle. Will need another 3 months

4 Yeasts   It is important to use the correct yeast for the type of wine to be made, as some yeasts have a higher alcoholic tolerance than others. When making sweet or dessert wines especially, always use a yeast suitable for the purpose. As already noted it is best to use yeasts in tablet or cultured form, since with drums there is a risk of deterioration if they are exposed to the air or kept too long in storage.

5 Sugar   As the yeast cells are inhibited by sugar in solution it is necessary to build up a strong colony of yeast cells before adding too much sugar. If the mistake has already been made, however, the only satisfactory remedy is to restart the fermentation.

Make a starter bottle (see p. 25), then check the quantity of sugar added to the 'stuck' must. If this was more than 2½ lb (1.1 k) plus a total of 3 lb (1.4 k) of fruit the quantity was above the alcoholic tolerance of the yeast and will need diluting with water. Take 1 pint (568 ml) of the must and 1 pint (568 ml) of cold water and pour into another demijohn with the active yeast starter; plug with cotton wool. When the fermentation is active add another pint of must and ½ pint water; when again active gradually add the remaining must and fit an airlock.

As dilution with water will have increased the volume of must to more than a gallon, the fermenting surplus can be placed in a bottle with a neck wide enough to take a bung and airlock; a milk bottle (the old type) or soft drinks bottle is ideal. This can be used for topping up at a later stage.

Yeast haze

In the normal way as the wine completes its fermentation the thick haze caused by the yeast cells will gradually sink to the bottom of the jar, building up a heavy deposit. If the specific gravity has dropped to 990 or below rack the wine, leave for two days and rack again, adding the recommended amount of Campden tablets or sodium or potassium metabisulphite. This should eliminate any remaining yeasts.

Pectin haze

Hazes caused by pectin can be prevented in the preparation stage by adding a pectin-destroying enzyme (see p. 21). If in doubt a simple test can be carried out to establish whether pectin is present. Take 1 tablespoon of wine, place it in a small bottle or glass and add three times the amount of methylated spirit, giving the bottle or glass a quick swirl. If a gelatinous clot forms, pectin is present. This may be remedied at this stage by adding one of the pectin-destroying enzymes, preferably a liquid one, using the amount recommended on the manufacturer's instructions. Leave for a few days to allow to settle before racking again.

Protein haze

Many wines made with a large proportion of fruit often show a fine haze caused by protein instability. In red wine the high tannin content helps precipitation by coagulating proteins that are in suspension. White wines are often more difficult to clear, however, and fruity type wines need a longer period in bulk to mature. If they fail to clear after twelve months some action can be taken. A short spell in a cold temperature of under 35°F (1°C) will often help, but if a stubborn protein haze remains a small amount of Bentonite (1 g per gallon of wine, see p. 35) should stabilise it. Pour the Bentonite liquid into the wine and stir thoroughly until well mixed. If the wine fails to clear after one week it may be necessary to resort to a gelatine and tannin fining: use ½ g gelatine and ¼ g tannin per gallon.

Many stubborn hazes can successfully be cleared by the addition of some banana liquid. Use 1 lb (500 g) of very ripe bananas, peeled and thinly sliced. Boil them for twenty minutes, strain and cool before adding 1 teaspoon (5 ml) of liquid pectin-destroying enzyme. Add 5 fl oz (142 ml) of the liquid to each gallon, blending thoroughly. Leave for a few days before racking. This treatment is very satisfactory for medium and sweet wines, but care should be taken not to exceed the dose in dry wines as it may alter their character.

Tartrates

This deposit occurs during the maturing period of red and white wines. The crystals form a deposit at the bottom of the jar, and in red wines they are encrusted with particles of colouring material. Their precipitation can be hastened by storing the wine in a cool place or placing it in the refrigerator for a few days. The wine is rarely cloudy as a result.

Enzymatic oxidation

Wines made from over-ripe fruit may be affected by an enzyme which accelerates the oxidation of tannins, causing a chocolate brown haze followed by a yellowish-brown deposit in red wines and a deep golden haze with a slight deposit in whites. In both cases the wines will taste and smell 'maderised', i.e. like caramel or burnt sugar. Once the wines have changed their character in this way there is no cure. Preventive measures are essential:

(a) the correct use of sulphur dioxide;
(b) care in racking;
(c) maintaining jars to full capacity after fermentation ceases.

Hydrogen sulphide

This, noticed as a smell of bad eggs, is frequently caused by using sulphite to stop a fairly vigorous fermentation. The fermenting yeasts will endeavour to reduce the sulphur dioxide to hydrogen sulphide, leaving the notorious smell. Wines should always be racked once to reduce the colony of active yeast cells and left in a cool place for two days before being racked again with the added sulphite. If the problem does occur it may be cured by adding a further 2 Campden tablets or 2 teaspoons (10 ml) of strong sulphite solution which will break up the hydrogen sulphide eventually precipitating it out. Wines afflicted with this problem will however lose much of their character.

Malolactic fermentation

In wines with a high malic acid content a secondary fermentation may occur, due to the action of lactobacilli breaking down the malic acid to form lactic acid and carbon dioxide. Some winemakers like to encourage this as it reduces the total acid present and the lactic acid formed is of a smoother nature. Care should be taken to sulphite the wine lightly (3 ml strong sulphite solution or ½ Campden tablet) to prevent other associated spoilage bacteria developing, particularly in low acid wines.

The bacteria which cause this fermentation are anaerobic, that is they are able to live without free oxygen from the air; they usually occur about nine months after vinification, especially if the storage temperature reaches 65–68°F (18–20°C).

Wines containing residual sugar should not be allowed to undergo a malolactic fermentation as strains of the bacteria are able to transform the sugars into lactic acid, acetic acid and mannitol, resulting in a bitter flavour. All sweet wines must therefore have extra sulphite added before storage and bottling, and the acid levels should be reasonably high as an added protection.

Another anaerobic bacteria forms a 'cotton wool' suspension and deposit, although the wine remains bright and clear. This should be controlled by a strong dose of sulphite (3 crushed Campden tablets or 3 teaspoons, 15 ml, of strong sulphite solution) and filtered after a few days.

Other diseases, such as Tourne which has a silky sheen when swirled against a strong light, and Ropiness, can be prevented by sulphite and the correct amount of acidity.

Acetification

Wines affected by bacteria that rely on oxygen from the air (aerobic) can rarely be saved in an advanced stage. The 'Wine to Vinegar' bacterium is undoubtedly the most common. Wines left exposed to the air can be infected by these bacteria, called Acetobacters, which infect the wine, using the oxygen present to convert some of the alcohol to acetaldhyde and finally to acetic acid. In the early stages the wine has an oily appearance on its surface and an acrid smell, which develops to a pronounced vinegar smell. Unless detected in the early stages very little can be done to save it. A wine with a slight infection may be treated with a strong dose of sulphite: 3 Campden tablets or 3 teaspoons (15 ml) of strong sulphite solution. The wine should then be filtered; it will not be of high quality, but may be used in punches, flavoured with herbs or spices.

Flowers of Wine (Fleur)

This infection becomes apparent from a thin layer of pink-grey mould which forms on the surface of the wine. The bacteria break down not only the alcohol but part of the fixed and volatile acidity, the dry extract and a certain amount of glycerine, resulting in a wine that is generally lacking life and vigour in both bouquet and taste. Again the treatment is a strong dose of sulphite solution or Campden tablets.

Care should be taken when racking this infected wine to keep the end of the syphon tube well below the surface mould to prevent any being carried over into the clean jar. The wine is only worth saving if the infection is discovered in the early stages.

Cleanliness at all stages, with a rational use of sulphite plus attention to regular topping up of the jars to exclude excessive amounts of oxygen, should prevent this malady.

'Off' flavours

As the wine clears the yeast cells and other insoluble matter drop to the bottom of the storage jar, forming a heavy deposit known as the lees. If this debris is allowed to decompose certain nitrogenous substances will be liberated into the wine, causing unpleasant flavours. The malaise known as 'mousiness' (i.e. a mousy smell) is caused by certain lactic bacteria and is apparent when a little wine is rubbed onto the hand and sniffed. There is no cure for this problem and care should be taken to sterilise thoroughly all equipment used. It is most important to rack as soon as fermentation has ceased and again when a heavy deposit appears.

Metallic hazes

These occur only if the must and wine have been in contact with any metal other than stainless steel. A common cause of this problem is the use of tinned ingredients when the tin has been damaged and the protective inner seal broken. In this case a whitish tint appears in white wines and a metallic blue tint in red wines. The addition of 5 g of citric acid per gallon of wine will usually prevent further development of the problem, but the haze will not disperse and the wine should be filtered.

This list of potential problems may appear alarming, but you will only occasionally meet any of them if you take heed of the basic principles:
1 Ensure cleanliness of utensils at all times
2 Use only high-quality ingredients
3 Take care to prevent oxidation in must and wine
4 Use sulphite as necessary (Campden tablets or sodium or potassium metabisulphite)
5 Maintain acid levels
6 Check temperature, chemical additives (pectin enzymes, nutrients) and sugar during fermentation
7 Use only plastic or stainless steel containers for preparation and glass for storage
8 Rack as soon as a heavy deposit appears
9 Top up storage jars.

Serving Wine

There is always an air of expectancy in selecting and opening a bottle of wine; if it has been made and stored correctly this will be confirmed when the cork is pulled.

Choosing the right type of wine for the occasion is an art in itself. First make sure that the wine is fully matured. The light flower and low-acid wines can be drunk when they are no more than six months old, while the average fruit wine will need at least twelve months. Young red wines are often harsh owing to their high tannin content and, except for wines that were pasteurised in the preparation stage, will need at least one or two years to mature. The full-bodied deep reds take several years to mellow and improve in character. The high tannin content improves the keeping qualities of these wines and they will remain in peak condition for several years. Dessert wines, owing to their high fruit and acid content, will also need to be stored for at least two years. It is often said that the last bottle in the batch is the best.

Expertise in presenting your wine will enhance its appeal, whatever the occasion. If you are giving a dinner party it is usual to start with a light white wine which will not cloy the palate, thus obscuring the lightness of the first course. White wines are best served cool, about 50°F (10°C), but they should not be over-chilled or they will lose some of their flavour and bouquet. As the meal proceeds, heavier white or red wines will complement the food. Red wines should be served at room temperature, about 60–65°F (16–18°C). If a quality wine has been stored for a long period it should be decanted, as this not

only ensures that the wine is free from any sediment but allows it to 'breathe' – i.e. to absorb oxygen which reacts with the wine, enhancing its flavour and bouquet. The length of time the wine should be left in the decanter varies, but generally the lighter red wines will need about half an hour and the full-bodied reds an hour. Well-made sweet wines can be enchanting and complement the dessert course, but for cheese it is better to stay with the reds.

At a social gathering the medium dry white and red wines are popular, and these too will be enhanced if served at the correct temperature as described above. For a wine to be drunk on its own it must be good, but no matter how much care you have taken there will always be the lesser wines. These are suitable for drinking as everyday family wines, or if the alcoholic strength is adequate they make a good base for a party punch, when flavourings and herbs will mask their lesser qualities.

The type of glasses chosen for serving wine play an important part. Plain clear glasses are preferable, as coloured and heavily engraved glasses distract attention from the wine. Make sure the glasses are sparkling clean so that when the wine is poured it reflects its true clarity and colour. Wine glasses should preferably be generous in size so that they are only filled to two-thirds their capacity. This allows the bouquet to develop on top of the wine. For sparkling wines tall flute-type glasses are best as this shape will slow down the release of the tiny bubbles of carbon dioxide caused by the decomposition of ethyl pyrocarbonate into carbon dioxide and alcohol.

Whatever the occasion – family anniversaries, parties with friends, summer outings and barbecues or cold winter's evenings by the fire – it will unfailingly be enriched by sharing a bottle of home-made wine.

BASIC WINEMAKING TECHNIQUE

If you have never made wine before it is a good idea to make a practical start using one of the grape concentrates, and as the process of fermentation gets under way the techniques described in other sections of the book will be more readily understood.

You will need to buy a few simple items of equipment to start with; some firms supply a 'Beginner's Kit'. The basic requirements are:

Two glass gallon jars, called demijohns
One plastic wine bucket with lid
A bored bung with an airlock
A bung to seal jar when fermentation ceases
A plastic funnel and sieve
A piece of plastic tubing about 6 feet (2 metres) long
Wine bottles and corks
1 tin of grape concentrate
1 bottle of Campden tablets
1 bottle or tub of pectin-destroying enzyme
1 bottle of Vit B$_1$ tablets
Wine yeast and yeast nutrient.

Other utensils necessary, such as a wooden or stainless steel spoon and a Pyrex measuring jug, are usually to be found in the kitchen.

First the yeast must be activated. Wash a small bottle (about ½ pint in size) and sterilise by boiling it for 15 minutes. Cool and half fill the bottle with cooled boiled water, add the juice of ½ lemon (25 ml) and 2 teaspoons (10 g) of sugar. Shake the mixture well and add 1 tablet or a sachet of wine yeast. Plug the top of the bottle with cotton wool and leave in a warm place (about

starter bottle

65–70°F, 18–21°C). After 24 hours bubbles should be rising rapidly to the surface as the yeast colony builds up.

Now prepare the demijohn by washing it thoroughly and draining. Crush 2 Campden tablets in 1 pint of tepid water and pour this into the demijohn. Place a bung in position and shake the jar well so that the liquid covers the inside of the jar; leave for 15 minutes. Remove the bung, place it with the airlock and

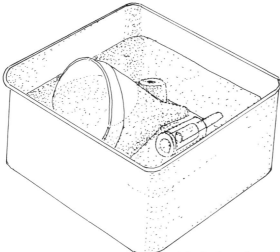

airlock, funnel and bung in sterilising solution

funnel in a bowl and pour the Campden tablet solution over them. Wash the demijohn thoroughly with cold water to remove any traces of the Campden solution.

Half fill the demijohn with cold boiled water and empty in the contents of the tin of grape concentrate. Swirl the liquid to distribute the concentrate evenly and pour in the active yeast starter. Plug fairly tightly with cotton wool. After 24 hours the fermentation should be quite active. Many of the instructions given for concentrates advocate the addition of sugar; if this is so, or if the fermentation is very active, dissolve the required amount of sugar in a pint of warm water and pour into the demijohn. The jar at this stage should be seven-eighths full. The airlock should now be pushed into the holed bung, and a little Campden tablet solution be added to the airlock to ensure a good seal. Push the bung tightly into the neck of the demijohn and stand this in a warm place. As the yeast colony builds up the liquid will become more cloudy, and the released gas bubbles will push their way through the airlock causing a rapid plopping sound. When the first vigorous fermentation subsides (usually after about three days) the demijohn should be topped up with cold boiled water. After about two weeks the fermentation will gradually decrease, and you will notice the slowing down of the bubbles passing through the airlock until finally they cease altogether. The wine should then be racked following the instructions on p. 33.

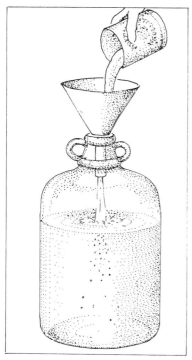

pour grape concentrate into boiled water and add yeast

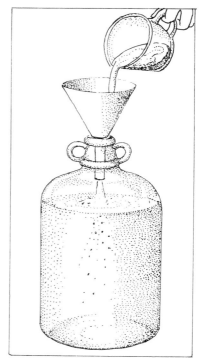

add sugar syrup after 24 hours

After you have made your first 'kit' wine proceed by adding some fresh fruit juices to the next one. Just half a pint of extracted juice will improve the result, although the wine will need storing for a little longer owing to the increased acidity. The juice from apples, grapes and gooseberries is suitable for white wines and that from blackberries, loganberries, currants, bilberries or elderberries for red. If you do not have a juice extractor, crush or liquidise the fruit in a pint of water before straining it into the jar.

Once you have mastered the basic process you should find little difficulty in proceeding to other country wines. The flower ones are easy to make and quick to mature, but do not miss the opportunity of storing or freezing some of the summer and autumn fruits. Always keep a record of the ingredients and the date on a label tied to each jar. It is also advisable to keep a detailed record sheet (see p. 39) filed away for future reference.

fit airlock

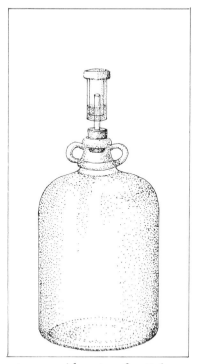

top up with water after 3 days

RECIPES

Certain points and procedures relevant to all the wines within a section are given in detail only in the first recipe of that section; these are printed in italic so that they may easily be referred to.

Quantities are given in imperial measurements. A brief metric guide appears throughout the recipe pages, and a full conversion table may be found on p. 124.

The pint measurement given for flowers represents as many petals (without the calyx and stalk) as will fit comfortably into a pint pot.

All recipes are for making one gallon of wine. Larger quantities should be made to the same proportions.

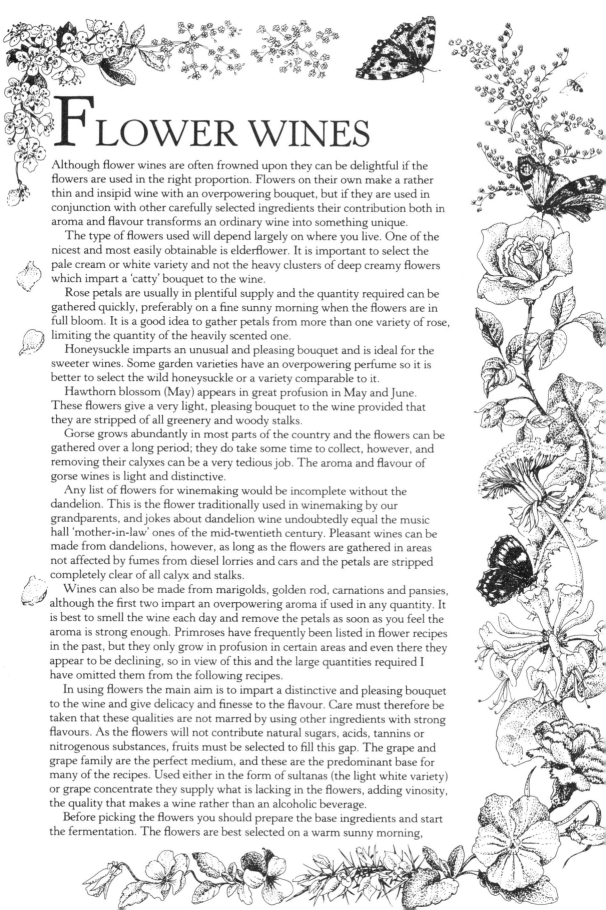

FLOWER WINES

Although flower wines are often frowned upon they can be delightful if the flowers are used in the right proportion. Flowers on their own make a rather thin and insipid wine with an overpowering bouquet, but if they are used in conjunction with other carefully selected ingredients their contribution both in aroma and flavour transforms an ordinary wine into something unique.

The type of flowers used will depend largely on where you live. One of the nicest and most easily obtainable is elderflower. It is important to select the pale cream or white variety and not the heavy clusters of deep creamy flowers which impart a 'catty' bouquet to the wine.

Rose petals are usually in plentiful supply and the quantity required can be gathered quickly, preferably on a fine sunny morning when the flowers are in full bloom. It is a good idea to gather petals from more than one variety of rose, limiting the quantity of the heavily scented one.

Honeysuckle imparts an unusual and pleasing bouquet and is ideal for the sweeter wines. Some garden varieties have an overpowering perfume so it is better to select the wild honeysuckle or a variety comparable to it.

Hawthorn blossom (May) appears in great profusion in May and June. These flowers give a very light, pleasing bouquet to the wine provided that they are stripped of all greenery and woody stalks.

Gorse grows abundantly in most parts of the country and the flowers can be gathered over a long period; they do take some time to collect, however, and removing their calyxes can be a very tedious job. The aroma and flavour of gorse wines is light and distinctive.

Any list of flowers for winemaking would be incomplete without the dandelion. This is the flower traditionally used in winemaking by our grandparents, and jokes about dandelion wine undoubtedly equal the music hall 'mother-in-law' ones of the mid-twentieth century. Pleasant wines can be made from dandelions, however, as long as the flowers are gathered in areas not affected by fumes from diesel lorries and cars and the petals are stripped completely clear of all calyx and stalks.

Wines can also be made from marigolds, golden rod, carnations and pansies, although the first two impart an overpowering aroma if used in any quantity. It is best to smell the wine each day and remove the petals as soon as you feel the aroma is strong enough. Primroses have frequently been listed in flower recipes in the past, but they only grow in profusion in certain areas and even there they appear to be declining, so in view of this and the large quantities required I have omitted them from the following recipes.

In using flowers the main aim is to impart a distinctive and pleasing bouquet to the wine and give delicacy and finesse to the flavour. Care must therefore be taken that these qualities are not marred by using other ingredients with strong flavours. As the flowers will not contribute natural sugars, acids, tannins or nitrogenous substances, fruits must be selected to fill this gap. The grape and grape family are the perfect medium, and these are the predominant base for many of the recipes. Used either in the form of sultanas (the light white variety) or grape concentrate they supply what is lacking in the flowers, adding vinosity, the quality that makes a wine rather than an alcoholic beverage.

Before picking the flowers you should prepare the base ingredients and start the fermentation. The flowers are best selected on a warm sunny morning, after the dew has risen and before the sun dries out the volatile oils. They should be placed in an open container, and never smothered in a plastic bag or left until the next day but processed on the day they are collected. Care must be taken to remove all the green calyx and stalk. The larger petals may need breaking or crushing before being added to the supplementary fermentation used to make the wine.

Do not boil or add boiling water to the petals as the volatile substances will easily vaporise and be dissipated in the steam. Some people will doubtless wonder about the quantity of bacteria these unwashed, unsulphited petals will bring to the wine. Provided that the flowers are selected from an area where there is not a build-up of pollution and are processed quickly and placed into the fermenting must in the container or jar, the build-up of carbon dioxide given off by the fermenting must will cut off their supply of oxygen, thus reducing the possibility of bacterial growth.

Elderflower 1

Sulphite for sterilising   *Dissolve 8 Campden tablets or ½ oz sodium or potassium metabisulphite in 2 pints water and store in a screw-topped bottle.*
Strong sulphite solution   *Add 1 oz sodium or potassium metabisulphite to ½ pint water. Store in a screw-topped bottle.*
Yeast starter bottle   *Sterilise a small bottle either by boiling for 20 minutes or filling with sterilising sulphite and leaving for 20 minutes. Pour back into the storage bottle and rinse twice to remove any sulphite solution. Half fill the bottle with cool boiled water, add the juice from half a lemon, 2 teaspoons granulated sugar and the wine yeast. Shake the bottle, plug with cotton wool and leave in a warm place (65–70°F, 18–21°C) for 48 hours.*

¼ pint elderflowers	1 teaspoon pectin-destroying enzyme
1½ lb white sultanas	1 teaspoon yeast nutrient
1½ lb sugar	1 Vit B₁ tablet
4 fl oz lemon juice or ¼ oz citric acid	Hock or Chablis type yeast
Water to 1 gallon	Campden tablets or strong sulphite solution

Activate the yeast starter bottle   Start records
Sterilise all equipment as required   *Prepare the covered plastic bucket and utensils by washing thoroughly with warm water. Place the utensils to be used in the bucket; pour in the sterilising solution. Replace lid tightly and swirl the solution around, making sure that it reaches all parts of the bucket. Leave for 20 minutes (longer if possible) before returning the solution to the storage bottle. It will remain effective for quite a long while providing it retains its pungent odour. Carefully wash the bucket and utensils with tap water to remove all traces of sulphite before use.*

Wash the sultanas thoroughly in warm water to remove the edible mineral oil; either mince or lightly liquidise in 5 pints of cold water and place in a plastic bucket with ½ crushed Campden tablet or 3 ml strong sulphite solution. Add the lemon juice, pectin-destroying enzyme, yeast nutrient and Vit B₁ tablet. Stir well and leave for 24 hours, tightly covering the bucket. Add the yeast starter, carefully pouring to one side of the bucket to enable a colony of active yeast cells to become established. When the colony is fully established it can be stirred into the bulk.

After 24 hours the fermentation should be very active, and the sultanas will then be forced to the top of the liquid by the carbon dioxide released. Choose a plate about the same size in diameter as the surface of the fermenting must. Sterilise it and place upside down on top of the must. If the fermentation is

Weight	
4 lb	1.8 k
1 lb	453 g
½ lb	226 g
1 oz	30 g
1 teaspoon	5 g

Liquid measure	
1 gallon	4.5 l
1 pint	568 ml
½ pint	284 ml
1 fluid oz	28 ml
1 teaspoon	5 ml

active it will stay firmly in place. Not only does this prevent excessive oxygen coming into contact with the must, it also ensures a quicker and more complete extraction as the particles of fruit are in contact with the fermenting liquid and this prevents them from drying out. The plate is also always available to break up the 'cap' of fruit when necessary. This should be done at least two or three times daily.

At this stage the flowers can be picked, processed and added to the fermenting must. In order that all the sugars, acids, tannin and nutrients from the fruit and bouquet and flavour from the flowers are extracted the fermentation should proceed on the pulp for about 3 days, depending on its activity. It should then be strained through a straining bag and poured into a clean demijohn. Again always take care to wash out the jar thoroughly with cold water after using the sulphite solution or the fermentation may be severely checked.

Pour as much liquid from the initial straining as possible into the demijohn. The remaining liquid from the straining bag can be added when it has drained free. Do not leave it too long or oxidation and contamination could occur. Dissolve the sugar by heating it in 1 pint of water; when cool pour into the demijohn.

Fit an airlock, using a little sulphite solution in the airlock first to ensure a good seal. Stand the demijohn in a warm place of 65–70°F (18–21°C) to ferment. Top up with a little water when the initial vigorous fermentation subsides.

When the fermentation ceases (usually about 2–3 weeks) syphon the clearing wine from the sediment into a clean demijohn and move to a cool place. After 1 or 2 days rack again, adding 2 Campden tablets or 2 teaspoons of strong sulphite solution; top up with a little cold water and store in a cool place. After 2 weeks rack again, adding 1 more Campden tablet or 1 teaspoon strong sulphite solution. Replace the airlock with a cork bung. Rack again when a heavy deposit forms.

Note *If you like there to be a little residual sugar in the wine, you should rack it when the S.G. drops to 1.000. In this way the sugars remaining in the wine will be glucose and fructose. Remove the wine to a cool place or refrigerate for 24 hours before racking again and adding the Campden tablets or strong sulphite solution. To safeguard this medium style wine an extra Campden tablet or 1 teaspoon strong sulphite solution should be added during the maturing period. If a little sweeter wine is required it may be necessary to add 2–4 oz sugar at this stage.*

Care must be taken not to add sulphite if the fermentation is very active, as the yeast enzymes will convert the sulphite to hydrogen sulphide. The wine must be racked off from the active yeast cells before adding sulphite.

Elderflower 2

Sulphite for sterilising
Strong sulphite solution
Yeast starter bottle

¼ pint elderflowers
1 can white grape concentrate (2.2 lb, 1 k)
½ lb sugar
Water to 1 gallon

1 teaspoon pectin enzyme
1 teaspoon yeast nutrient
1 Vit B_1 tablet
Graves or Bordeaux style yeast
Campden tablets or strong sulphite
   solution

Activate the yeast starter bottle   **Start records**
Sterilise all equipment as required

Add the pectin enzyme, yeast nutrient and Vit B_1 tablet to 5 pints of cold water. Stir vigorously until these ingredients are dissolved. Blend in the grape concentrate and the active yeast starter and pour into a demijohn, plugging the top with cotton wool. When the fermentation is active replace the cotton wool with an airlock. After the first vigorous fermentation subsides (usually about 3 days) pick the flowers, carefully remove the petals and drop them into the demijohn. Add the dissolved sugar, replace the airlock and ferment for a week before straining off the petals. Return the must to the demijohn to complete fermentation. Proceed as *in **Elderflower 1**.

Mature in bulk for 4 months before bottling. The wine is improved if left with a little residual sugar.

Elderflower 3

Sulphite for sterilising
Strong sulphite solution
Yeast starter bottle

¼ pint elderflowers
1½ lb white sultanas
2 lb mixed apples
2 fl oz lemon juice or 1 teaspoon citric acid
1¼ lb sugar
Water to 1 gallon

1 teaspoon pectin enzyme
1 teaspoon yeast nutrient
1 Vit B_1 tablet
Graves or Bordeaux type yeast
Campden tablet or strong sulphite
   solution

Activate the yeast starter bottle   **Start records**
Sterilise all equipment as required

Wash, chop or crush the apples and quickly place in the plastic bucket with 5 pints of cold water, 1 crushed Campden tablet or 1 teaspoon strong sulphite solution and the lemon juice. Add the thoroughly washed sultanas either minced or lightly liquidised, the pectin enzyme, yeast nutrient and Vit B_1 tablet. Stir well, cover with a plate to keep the fruit submerged and leave for 24 hours. Add the active yeast starter and ferment on the pulp for 3 days. Strain, pour into the demijohn with the flower petals and dissolved sugar. Fit an airlock and ferment for 1 week before straining off the flower petals. Return the must to the demijohn to complete fermentation. Proceed as *in **Elderflower 1**.

Mature in bulk for 6 months before bottling.

Elderflower 4

Sulphite for sterilising
Strong sulphite solution
Yeast starter bottle

¼ pint elderflowers
1½ lb white sultanas
¾ lb gooseberries
3 ripe bananas
1¼ lb sugar
Water to 1 gallon

1 teaspoon pectin enzyme
1 teaspoon yeast nutrient
1 Vit B_1 tablet
Graves or Bordeaux type yeast
Campden tablets or strong sulphite
   solution

Activate the yeast starter bottle   **Start records**
Sterilise all equipment as required

Wash the sultanas to remove all edible oil, wash the gooseberries and liquidise both fruits lightly. Put n a plastic bucket with 5 pints of cold water, 1 crushed Campden tablet or 1 teaspoon strong sulphite solution, the pectin enzyme, yeast nutrient and Vit B_1 tablet. Thinly slice the bananas and boil in 1 pint of water for 20 minutes, strain the cooled liquid into the fruit pulp. Stir, cover and leave for 24 hours. Add the active yeast starter, keep the fruit submerged with a plate and the bucket tightly covered. When the fermentation is active pick the flowers and add the petals to the must. Ferment on the pulp for a further 3 days. Strain, pressing the pulp lightly, and pour into a demijohn adding the dissolved sugar. Proceed as *in **Elderflower 1**.

Mature in bulk for 8 months before bottling. The wine is improved if left with a little residual sugar.

Weight	
4 lb	1.8 k
1 lb	453 g
½ lb	226 g
1 oz	30 g
1 teaspoon	5 g

Liquid·measure	
1 gallon	4.5 l
1 pint	568 ml
½ pint	284 ml
1 fluid oz	28 ml
1 teaspoon	5 ml

Dandelion

Sulphite for sterilising
Strong sulphite solution
Yeast starter bottle

½ pint dandelion petals
1½ lb white sultanas
3 oranges
1 teaspoon malic acid
1½ lb sugar
Water to 1 gallon

1 teaspoon pectin enzyme
1 teaspoon yeast nutrient
1 Vit B_1 tablet
Graves or Bordeaux type yeast
Campden tablets or strong sulphite
   solution

Activate the yeast starter bottle   **Start records**
Sterilise all equipment as required

Wash the sultanas to remove all edible oil and mince or lightly liquidise in 5 pints of cold water. Add the juice from the oranges and a little finely grated peel from one orange (avoiding the white pith) and place in the plastic bucket with the malic acid, yeast nutrient, pectin enzyme, Vit B_1 tablet and active yeast starter. Stir and cover. When the fermentation is active pick the flowers and carefully remove the petals taking care to exclude the green calyx and stalks. Add the flower petals to the must and keep them and the fruit pulp submerged with a plate. Ferment on the pulp for 3 days. Strain, add the dissolved sugar and proceed as *in **Elderflower 1**.

   Mature in bulk for 6–8 months before bottling.

Gorse or broom

Sulphite for sterilising
Strong sulphite solution
Yeast starter bottle

¼ pint gorse or broom petals
1 lb white sultanas
1 lb ripe bananas
½ pint concentrated pineapple juice
1 teaspoon malic acid
1¼ lb sugar
Water to 1 gallon

1 teaspoon pectin enzyme
1 teaspoon yeast nutrient
1 Vit B_1 tablet
All-purpose yeast
Campden tablets or strong sulphite
   solution

Activate the yeast starter bottle   **Start records**
Sterilise all equipment as required

Wash the sultanas and mince or lightly liquidise in 4 pints of cold water; put in the plastic bucket with ½ crushed Campden tablet or 3 ml strong sulphite solution. Thinly slice the bananas and boil in 1 pint of water for 20 minutes; strain the liquid into the bucket. Add the pineapple juice, pectin enzyme, yeast nutrient, Vit B_1 tablet and malic acid. Stir, cover and leave for 24 hours. Add the active yeast starter and when the fermentation is well under way pick the flowers and add the petals to the must. Keep the fruit submerged with a plate and ferment on the pulp for 3 days. Strain, add the dissolved sugar and proceed as *in **Elderflower 1**.

   Mature in bulk for 8 months before bottling. The wine is improved by a little residual sugar.

Honeysuckle 1

Sulphite for sterilising
Strong sulphite solution
Yeast starter bottle

¼ pint honeysuckle petals
1 jar apple juice (approx. 1 litre)
1 pint rosé grape concentrate
¾ lb sugar
Water to 1 gallon

1 teaspoon pectin enzyme
1 teaspoon yeast nutrient
1 Vit B_1 tablet
Bordeaux type yeast
Campden tablets or strong sulphite
    solution

Activate the yeast starter bottle   Start records
Sterilise all equipment as required

Add the pectin enzyme, yeast nutrient and Vit B_1 tablet to 4 pints of cold water, stir vigorously until dissolved. Blend in the apple juice and grape concentrate and pour into the demijohn. Add the active yeast starter and plug the jar with cotton wool. When the fermentation is active pick the flowers and drop the crushed petals into the demijohn with the dissolved sugar. Fit an airlock and ferment for 4 days before straining off the petals. Return the must to the demijohn to complete fermentation. Proceed as *in **Elderflower 1**.

Mature in bulk for 6 months before bottling. The wine is improved by a little residual sugar.

Honeysuckle 2

Sulphite for sterilising
Strong sulphite solution
Yeast starter bottle

¼ pint honeysuckle petals
1 lb white sultanas
2 lb pears
2 fl oz lemon juice or 1 teaspoon malic acid
1½ lb sugar
Water to 1 gallon

1 teaspoon pectin enzyme
1 teaspoon yeast nutrient
1 Vit B_1 tablet
Graves type yeast
Campden tablets or strong sulphite
    solution

Activate the yeast starter bottle   Start records
Sterilise all equipment as required

Wash, chop or crush the pears and quickly place in the plastic bucket with 5 pints water, 1 crushed Campden tablet or 1 teaspoon strong sulphite solution and the lemon juice. Add the thoroughly washed sultanas, either minced or lightly liquidised, the pectin enzyme, yeast nutrient and Vit B_1 tablet. Stir well, cover with a plate and keep the bucket tightly covered. Leave for 24 hours before adding the active yeast starter. When the fermentation is active, pick the flowers and add the crushed petals to the must. Ferment on the pulp for 3 days, keeping the fruit submerged. Strain, pour into the demijohn with the dissolved sugar and proceed as *in **Elderflower 1**.

Mature in bulk for 6 months before bottling. The wine should be left with a little residual sugar.

Weight	
4 lb	1.8 k
1 lb	453 g
½ lb	226 g
1 oz	30 g
1 teaspoon	5 g

Liquid measure	
1 gallon	4.5 l
1 pint	568 ml
½ pint	284 ml
1 fluid oz	28 ml
1 teaspoon	5 ml

Rose 1

Sulphite for sterilising
Strong sulphite solution
Yeast starter bottle

½ pint scented rose petals
1½ lb ripe peaches
¾ pint white grape concentrate
1 teaspoon malic acid
1 lb sugar
3 ripe bananas
Water to 1 gallon

1 teaspoon pectin enzyme
1 teaspoon yeast nutrient
1 Vit B_1 tablet
Graves type yeast
Campden tablets or strong sulphite
   solution

Activate the yeast starter bottle   **Start records**
Sterilise all equipment as required

Wash and stone the peaches, crush them and place in a plastic bucket with 4
pints water, 1 crushed Campden tablet or 1 teaspoon strong sulphite solution
and the pectin enzyme. Peel and thinly slice the bananas and boil for 20
minutes in 1 pint water; strain liquid into the peach pulp. Leave for 24 hours.
Strain, add the yeast nutrient, Vit B_1 tablet, malic acid and grape concentrate.
Stir well and when blended pour into the demijohn with the active yeast starter.
Plug the top with cotton wool. When the fermentation is active pick the
flowers, drop the crushed petals into the demijohn and add the dissolved sugar.
Fit an airlock and ferment for four days before straining off the petals and
returning the must to the demijohn to complete the fermentation. Proceed as
*in **Elderflower 1**.

    Mature in bulk for 6 months before bottling. The wine is improved if left
with a little residual sugar.

Rose 2

Sulphite for sterilising
Strong sulphite solution
Yeast starter bottle

½ pint scented rose petals
1½ lb white sultanas
1 lb mixed summer fruits (red or white
   currants, gooseberries, raspberries)
1 lb sugar
Water to 1 gallon

1 teaspoon pectin enzyme
1 teaspoon yeast nutrient
1 Vit B_1 tablet
Bordeaux type yeast
Campden tablets or strong sulphite
   solution

Activate the yeast starter bottle   **Start records**
Sterilise all equipment as required

Wash the sultanas thoroughly and mince or lightly liquidise in 5 pints cold
water. Crush the summer fruits and add with 1 crushed Campden tablet or 1
teaspoon strong sulphite solution, the pectin enzyme, yeast nutrient and Vit B_1
tablet. Cover and leave for 24 hours. Add the active yeast starter and ferment
on the pulp for 1 day before adding the crushed rose petals. Keep the fruit
submerged with a plate and the bucket tightly covered. After 3 days strain and
pour into the demijohn with the dissolved sugar. Proceed as *in **Elderflower 1**.

    Mature 8 months before bottling. The wine is improved by a little residual
sugar.

Hawthorn blossom

½ pint flower petals; other ingredients and methods as **Elderflower 1**, **2** or **3**.

Carnation or pansy

½ pint flower petals; other ingredients and method as **Elderflower 2** and **3** or **Honeysuckle 2**.

Marigold or golden rod

¼ pint marigold petals or the orange trumpets of golden rod (take care not to include any stalk or green leaf); other ingredients and method as for **Dandelion**.

Weight	
4 lb	1.8 k
1 lb	453 g
½ lb	226 g
1 oz	30 g
1 teaspoon	5 g
Liquid measure	
1 gallon	4.5 l
1 pint	568 ml
½ pint	284 ml
1 fluid oz	28 ml
1 teaspoon	5 ml

Fruit wines

Undoubtedly fruit wines will take pride of place over all others, for the quantity and variety of suitable fruits offer more scope than any other type. With so many differing acid levels, sugar quantities and flavours the challenge for the winemaker is also greater: it enables one to prove one's expertise in producing well-balanced wines. Fruit forms the base for the whole range of types—aperitifs, dry table wines, medium sweet, dessert and sparkling wines. As the dry table and medium sweet wines are the most popular, most of the recipes will be of this type.

In our changing climate the seasons vary so considerably that each year's batch can range from vintage to non-vintage wine depending on the weather. During good summers the fruits contain a high proportion of sugars with less acid and in poor years the opposite applies. The winemaker should adjust his recipes slightly in the poor years by adding a little less of the acidic fruits but maintaining the body and quality of the wine by increasing the more bland ones. It is far better to blend the ingredients in the early stages so that they have time to harmonise, rather than blending the wines at a later stage.

The methods of fermentation are described fully on pp. 25–32, but each method is described in detail in one of the recipes in each section. It should be remembered that fermentation on the pulp, provided that the top of the must is protected to exclude the oxygen, will give a greater rate of extraction of all the main ingredients: sugars, acids, tannins, flavour and nitrogenous substances. The infusion in water method will not give nearly such a high extraction rate but is more suitable for the lighter white table wines. Pasteurisation will extract colour, flavour and a medium proportion of acids and tannin but the wines made in this way are early maturing and lack the quality and character of the deep reds. This method serves a very useful purpose, however, as the wines can be drunk after twelve months, whereas the other reds take two or three years to mature, and should preferably be left for longer.

In selecting fruits the emphasis must be on quality and ripeness. Undamaged fruits are useless if they are not fully ripe, for the sugar content will be low and the acids high; conversely fruits that are over-ripe with bacterial spoilage will rarely produce wines of great excellence. When picking wild fruits try to select areas free from heavy pollution and process the fruits as quickly as possible.

Some fruits present more problems than others to prepare; apples are particularly tricky owing to their fleshy nature. The simplest method is to use a juice extractor for small quantities or a fruit press for larger quantities (see pp. 31–2). A little sulphite—1 Campden tablet or 1 teaspoon strong sulphite solution to every 7 lb (3 k) of fruit—will safeguard the juice from oxidation. An alternative method is to cut the apples into small pieces and place them in a mild sulphite solution as quickly as possible. To make one gallon using 5–6 lb (2–2½ k) of apples add 1 Campden tablet or 1 teaspoon strong sulphite solution to 4 pints (2 l) water. Drop the apple pieces in the solution, add the pectin enzyme, cover and leave for 24 hours before adding the yeast etc.

A good extraction rate can also be achieved by placing the washed apples in the deep freeze for 24 hours before use. Thaw them out in a mild sulphite

solution (1 Campden tablet to 4 pints water), covering them with a weighted plate in order to prevent them floating. When thawed they can be squashed by hand very easily. It is essential for the fermentation to start rapidly after using this method as the cell tissues are damaged by freezing, leaving them prone to oxidation. Other fruits which benefit from freezing to obtain an easier and better extraction rate are all the stoned fruits, elderberries and gooseberries.

Sultanas are recommended in many of the recipes; most sultanas are dipped in an edible mineral oil which should be removed by washing them carefully in warm water and draining before use.

Recipes using bottled and canned fruits are also included; many of these wines will mature more quickly owing to their lower acid level, so care must be taken to add the correct amount of sulphite at the end of fermentation to protect them from bacterial infection.

Sweet wines need a higher proportion of sulphite than dry wines, as much of the sulphite is used up combining with sugars, acids and aldehydes to form bisulphite compounds which leave a considerably reduced quantity of free sulphur dioxide to protect the wine from bacterial infection.

Apple 1 (pulp fermentation)

Sulphite for sterilising *Dissolve 8 Campden tablets or ½ oz sodium or potassium metabisulphite in 2 pints cold water and store in a screw-topped bottle.*

Strong sulphite solution *Add 1 oz to ½ pint water. Store in a small screw-topped bottle.*

Yeast starter bottle *Sterilise a small bottle either by boiling for 20 minutes or filling with sterilising sulphite and leaving for 20 minutes. Pour back into the storage bottle and rinse twice with cold water. Half fill the bottle with cool boiled water, add the juice from half a lemon, 2 teaspoons granulated sugar and the wine yeast. Shake the bottle, plug the top with cotton wool and leave in a warm place (65–70°F, 18–21°C) for 48 hours.*

6 lb mixed apples	2 teaspoons pectin-destroying enzyme
1 lb sultanas	1 teaspoon yeast nutrient
1½ lb sugar	1 Vit B$_1$ tablet
Water to 1 gallon	Hock type yeast
	Campden tablets or strong sulphite solution

Activate the yeast starter bottle   **Start records**

Sterilise all equipment as required *Prepare the covered plastic bucket and utensils by washing thoroughly with warm water. Place the utensils to be used in the bucket; pour in the sterilising solution. Replace lid tightly and swirl the solution around making sure that it reaches all parts of the bucket. Leave for 20 minutes (longer if possible) before returning the solution to the storage bottle. It will remain effective for quite a long while providing it retains its pungent odour. Carefully wash the bucket and utensils with tap water to remove all traces of sulphite.*

Dissolve 1 crushed Campden tablet or 1 teaspoon strong sulphite solution in 4 pints of cold water, placing in a sterilised fermenting bucket. Chop or slice the apples thinly and put them quickly into the sulphited water. Add the washed, minced or lightly liquidised sultanas, the pectin-destroying enzyme, yeast

Weight	
4 lb	1.8 k
1 lb	453 g
½ lb	226 g
1 oz	30 g
1 teaspoon	5 g

Liquid measure	
1 gallon	4.5 l
1 pint	568 ml
½ pint	284 ml
1 fluid oz	28 ml
1 teaspoon	5 ml

nutrient and Vit B_1 tablet. Stir, place an upturned plate on top of the fruit and cover the bucket. Leave for 24 hours.

Make sure the yeast starter is fully active before pouring it carefully into one side of the bucket. Reserve some in the starter bottle, topping up with a little 'starter medium' as a safeguard in case the bulk fails to activate.

If the active yeast starter is kept to a small area in the bucket an active yeast colony will quickly become established, and can then be stirred into the bulk must. When it is fully active a fruit cap will form on top of the must; this should be kept submerged with a plate to enable a quicker and better extraction rate and to exclude as much oxygen as possible. The cap should be broken up two or three times daily depending on the activity of the fermentation. Ferment on the pulp for 4 days. Strain off the liquid, pressing the pulp lightly and pour into the demijohn adding the dissolved sugar.

The demijohn should not be more than seven-eighths full as sometimes excessive frothing occurs, thus wasting the must. Any surplus can be poured into a small bottle and tightly plugged with cotton wool or if the neck is large enough an airlock can be fitted. The surplus can be returned to the bulk when the fermentation has subsided or used for topping up at a later stage. Fit an airlock and stand the demijohn in a warm place. Top the jar up after a few days with the surplus must or a little cold water. When the fermentation ceases (usually about two or three weeks) syphon the clearing wine from the sediment into a clean demijohn and move to a cool place. After one or two days rack again, adding 2 Campden tablets or 2 teaspoons of strong sulphite solution, topping up with a little cold water. Store in a cool place. After 2 weeks rack again, adding one more Campden tablet or 1 teaspoon strong sulphite solution.

Replace the airlock with a cork bung. Rack again when a heavy deposit forms. If care is taken there should not be any need to add any further sulphite for dry table wines, but if in doubt another Campden tablet or 1 teaspoon strong sulphite solution may be added.

Note   *If you like there to be a little residual sugar in the wine, you should rack it when the S.G. drops to 1.000. Remove to a cool place or refrigerate for 24 hours before racking and adding the Campden tablets or strong sulphite solution. To safeguard this medium dry wine an extra Campden tablet or 1 teaspoon strong sulphite solution should be added during the maturing period.*

Apple 2 (juice extraction)

**Sulphite for sterilising
Strong sulphite solution
Yeast starter bottle**

3 pints apple juice
¾ pint white grape concentrate
2 fl oz lemon juice
1½ lb sugar
Water to 1 gallon

2 teaspoons pectin enzyme
1 teaspoon yeast nutrient
1 Vit B_1 tablet
Hock or Chablis type yeast
Campden tablets or strong sulphite solution

**Activate the yeast starter bottle   Start records
Sterilise all equipment as required**

When the yeast is active pour the apple juice, grape concentrate and lemon juice into a demijohn, adding the pectin-destroying enzyme, yeast nutrient, Vit

B$_1$ tablet and active yeast starter. Add a little water to increase the total liquid to 4 pints. For those who wish to monitor the fermentation process a hydrometer reading can be taken at this stage by pouring some liquid into the trial jar and inserting the hydrometer. If the S.G. reading is 1.080 for the *half gallon* it must be divided to give the S.G. for *one gallon*, i.e. S.G. 1.040. (This is because the additional half gallon would be water at S.G. 1.000).

In order to increase the S.G. to the required level of 1.090 sugar syrup will have to be added. As a rough guide 1 oz per gallon will increase the S.G. to 1.002, so in order to obtain an increase in S.G. of 1.050 the sugar requirement will be 25 oz (1 lb 9 oz, or 700 g).

Return the liquid from the trial jar to the demijohn, adding an extra 2 pints of cold water; plug the top of the jar with cotton wool. When the fermentation is active (usually about 24 hours) the dissolved sugar may be added. Fit an airlock, stand in a warm place and proceed as *in **Apple 1**.

Mature in bulk for 12 months before bottling.

Apple 3 (freezing)

Sulphite for sterilising
Strong sulphite solution
Yeast starter bottle

4 lb mixed apples
2 lb pears
1 lb white sultanas
1¾ lb sugar
Water to 1 gallon

2 teaspoons pectin enzyme
1 teaspoon yeast nutrient
1 Vit B$_1$ tablet
Hock or Chablis type yeast
Campden tablets or strong sulphite solution

Activate the yeast starter bottle   Start records
Sterilise all equipment as required

Wash the apples and pears and place in the deep freeze for 24 hours. Wash and mince or lightly liquidise the sultanas and put them in a plastic bucket with 5 pints of cold water and 1 crushed Campden tablet or 1 teaspoon strong sulphite solution, the pectin enzyme, yeast nutrient and Vit B$_1$ tablet. Remove the frozen apples and pears from the freezer and place in the liquid, weighting them down with a large heavy plate to keep them submerged. After 24 hours they can easily be crushed by hand. Add the active yeast starter and ferment on the pulp for 3 days, keeping the fruit cap submerged as far as possible with the upturned plate. Keep the bucket tightly covered. Strain, pour into the demijohn with the dissolved sugar and proceed as *in **Apple 1**.

Mature in bulk for 12 months before bottling.

Apple 4

Sulphite for sterilising
Strong sulphite solution
Yeast starter bottle

3 lb crab apples
1 lb fresh rosehips
1 lb sultanas
1¾ lb sugar
Water to 1 gallon

2 teaspoons pectin enzyme
1 teaspoon yeast nutrient
1 Vit B$_1$ tablet
Hock or Chablis type yeast
Campden tablets or strong sulphite solution

Activate the yeast starter bottle   Start records
Sterilise all equipment as required

Weight	
4 lb	1.8 k
1 lb	453 g
½ lb	226 g
1 oz	30 g
1 teaspoon	5 g

Liquid measure	
1 gallon	4.5 l
1 pint	568 ml
½ pint	284 ml
1 fluid oz	28 ml
1 teaspoon	5 ml

Crush the rosehips, finely chop or crush the crab apples and quickly place in the plastic bucket with 6 pints of cold water and 1 crushed Campden tablet or 1 teaspoon strong sulphite solution. Add the washed and minced sultanas, the pectin enzyme, yeast nutrient and Vit B_1 tablet. Cover with a plate and leave for 24 hours, keeping the bucket tightly covered. Add the active yeast starter and ferment on the pulp for 3 days. Strain, pour into the demijohn with the dissolved sugar and proceed as *in **Apple 1**.

Mature in bulk for 8–12 months before bottling. The wine may be racked when the S.G. drops to 1.000, leaving a little residual sugar.

Apple 5

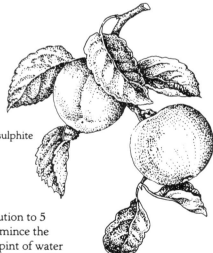

Sulphite for sterilising
Strong sulphite solution
Yeast starter bottle

2 pints apple juice
1 tin pineapple juice (approx. 1 pint)
¾ pint grape concentrate
½ lb bananas
1 lb sugar
Water to 1 gallon

1 teaspoon pectin enzyme
1 teaspoon yeast nutrient
1 Vit B_1 tablet
Hock or Chablis type yeast
Campden tablets or strong sulphite
   solution

Activate the yeast starter bottle   **Start records**
Sterilise all equipment as required

Boil the thinly sliced bananas in 1 pint of water for 20 minutes; drain off the liquid, discarding the pulp. When cool add the apple juice, pineapple juice, pectin enzyme, yeast nutrient, Vit B_1 tablet and active yeast starter. An S.G. reading can be taken at this stage if desired, following the instructions for **Apple 2**.

Pour into the demijohn, top up to three-quarters full with cold water and plug the top of the jar with cotton wool. When the fermentation is fully active add the dissolved sugar. Proceed as *in **Apple 1**.

Mature in bulk for 6 months before bottling.

Apricot 1

Sulphite for sterilising
Strong sulphite solution
Yeast starter bottle

1 lb fresh apricots
1½ lb white sultanas
½ lb ripe bananas
1¼ lb sugar
Water to 1 gallon

1 teaspoon pectin enzyme
1 teaspoon yeast nutrient
1 Vit B_1 tablet
Hock or Chablis type yeast
Campden tablets or strong sulphite
   solution

Activate the yeast starter bottle   **Start records**
Sterilise all equipment as required

Add 1 crushed Campden tablet or 1 teaspoon strong sulphite solution to 5 pints of cold water. Stone the apricots and chop finely, wash and mince the sultanas and add to the liquid. Boil the thinly sliced bananas in 1 pint of water and add the strained liquid. Add the pectin enzyme, yeast nutrient and Vit B_1 tablet, stir well. Keep the fruit pulp submerged with a plate and the bucket tightly covered. After 24 hours add the active yeast starter and ferment on the pulp for 3 days. Strain, pour into the demijohn and add the dissolved sugar. Proceed as *in **Apple 1**.

Mature in bulk for 12 months before bottling.

Apricot 2

1 large tin apricots (lb 13 oz, 822 g)
1 lb gooseberries
1½ lb white sultanas
1¼ lb sugar
Water to 1 gallon

Sulphite for sterilising
Strong sulphite solution
Yeast starter bottle

1 teaspoon pectin enzyme
1 teaspoon yeast nutrient
1 Vit B_1 tablet
Hock or Chablis type yeast
Campden tablets or strong sulphite
    solution

Activate the yeast starter bottle   **Start records**
Sterilise all equipment as required

Put 1 crushed Campden tablet or 1 teaspoon of strong sulphite solution in 4
pints of cold water into a plastic bucket. Wash the sultanas and gooseberries,
mince the sultanas and crush the gooseberries, placing them in the water with
the pectin enzyme, yeast nutrient and Vit B_1 tablet. Cover and leave for 24
hours. Chop the apricots and add with their liquid to the other ingredients.
Carefully pour in the active yeast starter and ferment on the pulp for 3 days.
Strain, pour into the demijohn with the dissolved sugar and proceed as *in
Apple 1.
     Mature in bulk for 12 months before bottling.

Apricot 3

2 medium-sized tins apricots (2½ lb, 1.1 k)
2 lb apples
1 lb bananas
1 lb white sultanas
1¼ lb sugar
½ pint cream or yellow rose petals
Water to 1 gallon

Sulphite for sterilising
Strong sulphite solution
Yeast starter bottle

2 teaspoons pectin enzyme
1 teaspoon yeast nutrient
1 Vit B_1 tablet
Sauternes type yeast
Campden tablets or strong sulphite
    solution

Activate the yeast starter bottle   **Start records**
Sterilise all equipment as required

Put 1 crushed Campden tablet or 1 teaspoon of strong sulphite solution in 4
pints of cold water. Pour into a plastic bucket and add the chopped or crushed
apples and the washed minced sultanas. Thinly slice the bananas and boil in 1
pint of water for 20 minutes, adding the strained liquid. When cool add the
pectin enzyme, yeast nutrient and Vit B_1 tablet. Cover and leave for 24 hours.
Chop the apricots and add with their liquid to the other ingredients. Pour in
the activated yeast starter and when the fermentation is really active add the
crushed rose petals. Ferment on the pulp for 3 days. Strain and pour into the
demijohn, adding half the quantity of sugar and the remainder when the S.G.
drops to 1.005. The fermentation can be stopped when the S.G. again reaches
1.005 by racking into a clean jar and placing in the refrigerator for 24 hours.
Rack again, adding 3 Campden tablets or 3 teaspoons strong sulphite solution.
Rack again after 2 weeks.
     Mature in bulk for 12 months before bottling.

Weight	
4 lb	1.8 k
1 lb	453 g
½ lb	226 g
1 oz	30 g
1 teaspoon	5 g

Liquid measure	
1 gallon	4.5 l
1 pint	568 ml
½ pint	284 ml
1 fluid oz	28 ml
1 teaspoon	5 ml

Bilberry 1

Sulphite for sterilising
Strong sulphite solution
Yeast starter bottle

2 lb fresh bilberries
1 lb sultanas
½ lb dried currants
½ lb ripe bananas
4 fl oz lemon juice or 2 teaspoons citric acid
1¾ lb sugar
Water to 1 gallon

1 teaspoon pectin enzyme
1 teaspoon yeast nutrient
1 Vit B_1 tablet
Burgundy type yeast
Campden tablets or strong sulphite
solution

Activate the yeast starter bottle   **Start records**
Sterilise all equipment as required

Remove stalks, wash and crush the bilberries, wash the sultanas and currants and mince or lightly liquidise them, placing in a plastic bucket with 5 pints of cold water. Add the crushed Campden tablet or 1 teaspoon strong sulphite solution, the lemon juice, pectin enzyme, yeast nutrient and Vit B_1 tablet. Slice the bananas thinly and boil in ½ pint of water for 20 minutes, strain and when cool add to the other ingredients. Cover and leave for 24 hours. Add the active yeast starter and ferment on the pulp for 4 days, keeping the fruit submerged with an upturned plate and the bucket tightly covered. Strain and pour into the demijohn with the dissolved sugar. Proceed as *in **Apple 1**.

Mature in bulk for at least 12 months before bottling.

Bilberry 2 (pasteurised)

Sulphite for sterilising
Strong sulphite solution
Yeast starter bottle

2 × 1 lb jars bilberries
½ lb sloes or bullaces
½ lb dried currants
1 lb sultanas
1½ lb sugar
Water to 1 gallon

1 teaspoon pectin enzyme
1 teaspoon yeast nutrient
1 Vit B_1 tablet
Burgundy type yeast
Campden tablets or strong sulphite
solution

Activate the yeast starter bottle   **Start records**
Sterilise all equipment as required

Wash the currants and sultanas, mince or lightly liquidise and place in a large stainless steel saucepan with 4 pints of water. Add the crushed sloes or bullaces and heat to 150°F (65°C), maintaining this temperature for 5 minutes. When cool pour into a plastic bucket, adding the bilberries, pectin enzyme, yeast nutrient, Vit B_1 tablet and active yeast starter. Ferment on the pulp for 2 days, keeping the fruit submerged. Strain, pour into the demijohn and add the dissolved sugar. Proceed as *in **Apple 1**.

Mature in bulk for 8 months before bottling.

Blackberry 1

Sulphite for sterilising
Strong sulphite solution
Yeast starter bottle

2 lb blackberries
1 lb sloes, bullaces or blackcurrants
1½ lb sultanas
1¼ lb sugar
Water to 1 gallon

1 teaspoon pectin enzyme
1 teaspoon yeast nutrient
1 Vit B_1 tablet
Burgundy type yeast
Campden tablets or strong sulphite
    solution

Activate the yeast starter bottle   **Start records**
Sterilise all equipment as required

Wash and crush the blackberries and sloes, wash and mince the sultanas and place in a plastic bucket. Add 5 pints of cold water, 1 crushed Campden tablet or 1 teaspoon strong sulphite solution, the yeast nutrient, pectin enzyme and Vit B_1 tablet. Leave for 24 hours before adding the active yeast starter. Ferment on the pulp for 3 days, keeping the fruit submerged with a plate and the bucket tightly covered. Strain, pour into a demijohn with the dissolved sugar. Proceed as *in **Apple 1**.
    Mature in bulk for 12–18 months before bottling.

Blackberry 2

Sulphite for sterilising
Strong sulphite solution
Yeast starter bottle

2 lb blackberries
2 lb apples
2 lb pears
¾ pint red grape concentrate
1¼ lb sugar
Water to 1 gallon

1 teaspoon pectin enzyme
1 teaspoon yeast nutrient
1 Vit B_1 tablet
Burgundy type yeast
Campden tablets or strong sulphite
    solution

Activate the yeast starter bottle   **Start records**
Sterilise all equipment as required

Wash, chop or crush the apples and pears and place in a plastic bucket with 4 pints of cold water and 1 crushed Campden tablet or 1 teaspoon strong sulphite solution, the pectin enzyme, yeast nutrient and Vit B_1 tablet. Wash and crush the blackberries and add to the other fruit pulp, taking care to keep the fruit submerged with a plate and the bucket tightly covered. After 24 hours add the active yeast starter and ferment on the pulp for 3 days, still keeping the fruit submerged. Strain, pour into the demijohn, add the grape concentrate and the dissolved sugar and proceed as *in **Apple 1**.
    Mature in bulk for 12 months before bottling.

Weight	
4 lb	1.8 k
1 lb	453 g
½ lb	226 g
1 oz	30 g
1 teaspoon	5 g

Liquid measure	
1 gallon	4.5 l
1 pint	568 ml
½ pint	284 ml
1 fluid oz	28 ml
1 teaspoon	5 ml

Blackberry 3 (pasteurised)

Sulphite for sterilising
Strong sulphite solution
Yeast starter bottle

2 lb blackberries
1 lb elderberries
1 lb bananas
½ pint red grape concentrate
2 fl oz lemon juice
1½ lb sugar
Water to 1 gallon

1 teaspoon pectin enzyme
1 teaspoon yeast nutrient
1 Vit B₁ tablet
Burgundy type yeast
Campden tablets or strong sulphite
 solution

Activate the yeast starter bottle   **Start records**
Sterilise all equipment as required

De-stalk and wash the elderberries and blackberries, crush and place in a
stainless steel saucepan adding 4 pints of cold water. Heat to 150°F (65°C),
maintaining for 5 minutes. Boil the thinly sliced bananas in 1 pint of water for
20 minutes, add the strained liquid to the other ingredients. When cool add the
lemon juice, pectin enzyme, yeast nutrient and Vit B₁ tablet. Leave 24 hours
before straining and pressing the pulp. Pour into the demijohn with the active
yeast starter, plug the top with cotton wool. When fermentation is active add
the grape concentrate and dissolved sugar. Fit an airlock and ferment to
completion, then proceed as *in **Apple 1**.
  Store 18 months in bulk before bottling.

Blackcurrant 1

Sulphite for sterilising
Strong sulphite solution
Yeast starter bottle

2 lb blackcurrants
1 lb dried currants
½ lb sultanas
1 lb bananas
1¾ lb sugar
Water to 1 gallon

1 teaspoon pectin enzyme
1 teaspoon yeast nutrient
1 Vit B₁ tablet
Burgundy or Rhone type yeast
Campden tablets or strong sulphite
 solution

Activate the yeast starter bottle   **Start records**
Sterilise all equipment as required

Wash and crush the blackcurrants, wash the dried currants and sultanas; mince
or lightly liquidise them and place in a plastic bucket with 5 pints water, 1
crushed Campden tablet or 1 teaspoon strong sulphite solution, the pectin
enzyme, yeast nutrient and Vit B₁ tablet. Slice the bananas thinly and boil in 1
pint of water for 20 minutes; strain the cooled liquid over the other ingredients.
Leave for 24 hours before adding the active yeast starter. Ferment on the pulp
for 5 days, keeping the fruit submerged with a plate and the bucket tightly
covered. Strain and pour into a demijohn adding the dissolved sugar. Proceed
as *in **Apple 1**.
  Keep 18 months to 2 years in bulk before bottling.

Blackcurrant 2

Sulphite for sterilising
Strong sulphite solution
Yeast starter bottle

1½ lb blackcurrants
1 lb mixed summer fruits (raspberries,
    loganberries, garden blackberries,
    gooseberries, etc.)
1 lb sultanas
½ lb bananas
1½ lb sugar
Water to 1 gallon

2 teaspoons pectin enzyme
1 teaspoon yeast nutrient
1 Vit B_1 tablet
Burgundy type yeast
Campden tablets or strong sulphite
    solution

Activate the yeast starter bottle   **Start records**
Sterilise all equipment as required

Wash the fruits. Skin the bananas and crush or lightly liquidise them with the fruits in 5 pints of cold water and 1 crushed Campden tablet or 1 teaspoon strong sulphite solution. Add the pectin enzyme, yeast nutrient and Vit B_1 tablet and leave for 24 hours before adding the active yeast starter. Ferment on the pulp for 3 days, keeping the fruit submerged with a plate and the bucket tightly covered. Strain and pour into a demijohn, adding the dissolved sugar. Proceed as *in **Apple 1**.

    Mature in bulk for 18 months before bottling.

Cherry 1

Sulphite for sterilising
Strong sulphite solution
Yeast starter bottle

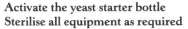

3 lb morello or Early River cherries
¾ pint red grape concentrate
1½ lb sugar
Water to 1 gallon

1 teaspoon pectin enzyme
1 teaspoon yeast nutrient
1 Vit B_1 tablet
Bordeaux type yeast
Campden tablets or strong sulphite
    solution

Activate the yeast starter bottle   **Start records**
Sterilise all equipment as required

Wash and crush the cherries, taking care not to break the stones; place them in a plastic bucket with 4 pints water and 1 crushed Campden tablet or 1 teaspoon strong sulphite solution, the pectin enzyme, yeast nutrient and Vit B_1 tablet. Leave 24 hours before adding the active yeast starter. Ferment on the pulp for 3 days, keeping the fruit submerged with a plate and the bucket tightly covered. Strain, pressing the pulp, and pour into the demijohn with the grape concentrate and the dissolved sugar. Proceed as *in **Apple 1**.

    The wine can be left with a little residual sugar if desired by racking when the S.G. drops to 1.000. Mature in bulk for 8 months before bottling.

Weight	
4 lb	1.8 k
1 lb	453 g
½ lb	226 g
1 oz	30 g
1 teaspoon	5 g

Liquid measure	
1 gallon	4.5 l
1 pint	568 ml
½ pint	284 ml
1 fluid oz	28 ml
1 teaspoon	5 ml

Cherry 2

Sulphite for sterilising
Strong sulphite solution
Yeast starter bottle

2 lb jar Krakus morello cherries
1 lb sloes or bullaces
1 lb sultanas
1½ lb sugar
Water to 1 gallon

1 teaspoon pectin enzyme
1 teaspoon yeast nutrient
1 Vit B_1 tablet
Bordeaux type yeast
Campden tablets or strong sulphite solution

Activate the yeast starter bottle   **Start records**
Sterilise all equipment as required

Wash and crush the sloes, taking care not to break the stones, wash and mince the sultanas and place in the plastic bucket with the cherries and 4 pints of cold water, 1 crushed Campden tablet or 1 teaspoon strong sulphite solution, the pectin enzyme, yeast nutrient and Vit B_1 tablet. Stir and leave for 24 hours before adding the active yeast starter. Ferment on the pulp for 3 days, keeping the fruit submerged with a plate and the bucket tightly covered. Strain, pressing the pulp, and pour into the demijohn adding the dissolved sugar. Proceed as *in **Apple 1**.

Mature in bulk for 12 months before bottling.

Cherry and grape

Sulphite for sterilising
Strong sulphite solution
Yeast starter bottle

3 lb morello or Early River cherries
7 lb black grapes
1¼ lb sugar
Water to 1 gallon

1 teaspoon pectin enzyme
1 teaspoon yeast nutrient
1 Vit B_1 tablet
Burgundy or Bordeaux type yeast
Campden tablets or strong sulphite solution

Activate the yeast starter bottle   **Start records**
Sterilise all equipment as required

Wash and crush the cherries and grapes and place them in a plastic bucket with 2 pints of water, 1 crushed Campden tablet or 1 teaspoon strong sulphite solution, the pectin enzyme, yeast nutrient and Vit B_1 tablet. Stir well, keep the fruit submerged and leave for 24 hours. Add the active yeast starter and ferment on the pulp for 6 days, keeping the fruit submerged with a plate and the bucket tightly covered. Strain, dissolve the sugar in the must and pour into the demijohn. Proceed as *in **Apple 1**.

Store 12 months before bottling.

This wine is rather expensive to make, so the cherries should be purchased and frozen until the cheaper grapes arrive in the autumn. Alternatively you can use two jars of cherries but the wine will lack a little vitality.

Damson 1 (pasteurised)

Sulphite for sterilising
Strong sulphite solution
Yeast starter bottle

3 lb damsons
½ lb bananas
¾ pint red grape concentrate
1½ lb sugar
Water to 1 gallon

1 teaspoon pectin enzyme
1 teaspoon yeast nutrient
1 Vit B₁ tablet
Burgundy type yeast
Campden tablets or strong sulphite
   solution

Activate the yeast starter bottle   Start records
Sterilise all equipment as required

Wash the damsons, break the skins and place in a stainless steel saucepan with
4 pints of cold water. Heat to 150°F (65°C), maintaining the heat for 5 minutes.
Thinly slice the bananas and boil in 1 pint of water for 20 minutes. Strain the
liquid into the damsons. When cool add the pectin enzyme, yeast nutrient and
Vit B₁ tablet. Leave 24 hours before straining. Pour into a demijohn with the
active yeast starter. Plug the top with cotton wool. When the fermentation is
active add the grape concentrate and the dissolved sugar and proceed as *in
Apple 1.
   Mature in bulk for 12 months before bottling. The wine may be racked
when the S.G. drops to 1.000, leaving a little residual sugar.

Damson 2

Sulphite for sterilising
Strong sulphite solution
Yeast starter bottle

3 lb damsons
1 lb dried currants
½ lb sultanas
2 fl oz lemon juice
1½ lb sugar
Water to 1 gallon

1 teaspoon pectin enzyme
1 teaspoon yeast nutrient
1 Vit B₁ tablet
Burgundy type yeast
Campden tablet or strong sulphite
   solution

Activate the yeast starter bottle   Start records
Sterilise all equipment as required

Boil 5 pints of water and pour over the slightly crushed damsons, the washed
and minced sultanas and currants. When cool add 1 crushed Campden tablet
or 1 teaspoon strong sulphite solution, the pectin enzyme, yeast nutrient, Vit B₁
tablet and lemon juice. Leave 24 hours before adding the active yeast starter.
Ferment on the pulp for 5 days, keeping the fruit submerged with a plate and
the bucket tightly covered. Strain carefully and pour the liquid into a demijohn
with the dissolved sugar. Proceed as *in **Apple 1**.
   Mature in bulk for 12–18 months before bottling.

Weight	
4 lb	1.8 k
1 lb	453 g
½ lb	226 g
1 oz	30 g
1 teaspoon	5 g

Liquid measure	
1 gallon	4.5 l
1 pint	568 ml
½ pint	284 ml
1 fluid oz	28 ml
1 teaspoon	5 ml

Elderberry 1

Sulphite for sterilising
Strong sulphite solution
Yeast starter bottle

2 lb elderberries
1 lb sloes, bullaces or blackcurrants
½ lb dried currants
1 lb sultanas
1½ lb sugar
Water to 1 gallon

1 teaspoon pectin enzyme
1 teaspoon yeast nutrient
1 Vit B_1 tablet
Burgundy or Bordeaux type yeast
Campden tablets or strong sulphite
    solution

**Activate the yeast starter bottle   Start records
Sterilise all equipment as required**

Strip the elderberries from the stems and wash them, removing any green ones that float to the surface. Crush the berries with the sloes, add the washed, minced dried currants and sultanas and place in a plastic bucket with 5 pints of cold water, 1 crushed Campden tablet or 1 teaspoon strong sulphite solution, the pectin enzyme, yeast nutrient and Vit B_1 tablet. Stir well and leave for 24 hours before adding the active yeast starter. Ferment on the pulp for 3 days, keeping the fruit submerged with a plate and the bucket tightly covered. Strain and pour into a demijohn with the dissolved sugar. Proceed as *in **Apple 1**.

Store in bulk for 18 months before bottling.

Elderberry 2 (pasteurised)

Sulphite for sterilising
Strong sulphite solution
Yeast starter bottle

2 lb elderberries
1 lb damsons
1 lb ripe bananas
¾ pint red grape concentrate
1½ lb sugar
Water to 1 gallon

1 teaspoon pectin enzyme
1 teaspoon yeast nutrient
1 Vit B_1 tablet
Burgundy or Bordeaux type yeast
Campden tablets or strong sulphite
    solution

**Activate the yeast starter bottle   Start records
Sterilise all equipment as required**

Strip the elderberries from the stems and wash them, removing any green ones that float to the surface. Crush the berries and place in a stainless steel saucepan with the damsons and 4 pints of cold water. Heat to 150°F (65°C), maintain for 5 minutes and remove from heat. Boil the thinly sliced bananas in 1 pint of water for 20 minutes, then drain the liquid into the other fruit. Strain the liquid, when cool add the pectin enzyme, yeast nutrient, Vit B_1 tablet and active yeast starter and pour into a demijohn, plugging the top with cotton wool. When fermentation is active add the grape concentrate and dissolved sugar. Proceed as *in **Apple 1**.

Mature in bulk for 12 months before bottling.

Elderberry 3

Sulphite for sterilising
Strong sulphite solution
Yeast starter bottle

2 lb elderberries
1 lb blackberries
2 lb pears
½ lb sultanas
3 fl oz lemon juice or
    ¼ oz tartaric acid
1¾ lb sugar
Water to 1 gallon

1 teaspoon pectin enzyme
1 teaspoon yeast nutrient
1 Vit B_1 tablet
Burgundy or Bordeaux type yeast
Campden tablets or strong sulphite
    solution

Activate the yeast starter bottle   Start records
Sterilise all equipment as required

Strip the elderberries from the stems and wash them, removing any green ones that float to the surface. Crush them with the blackberries and pour 4 pints boiling water over them. Stir for 5 minutes and strain off the juice. Repeat, using 1½ pints of boiling water, and press the pulp to extract as much juice as possible. When cool add 1 Campden tablet, the pectin enzyme, lemon juice, yeast nutrient and Vit B_1 tablet. Wash the pears, thinly slice or crush them, add with the washed minced sultanas to the juice. Keep the fruit submerged with a plate and the bucket tightly covered. After 24 hours add the active yeast starter and ferment on the pulp for 3 days, still keeping the fruit submerged. Strain and pour into a demijohn with the dissolved sugar. Proceed as *in **Apple 1**.
    Mature in bulk for 12 months before bottling.

Elderberry 4

Sulphite for sterilising
Strong sulphite solution
Yeast starter bottle

2 lb elderberries
4 lb black grapes
1 lb sultanas
¾ pint red grape concentrate
3 fl oz lemon juice
1¼ lb sugar
Water to 1 gallon

1 teaspoon pectin enzyme
Burgundy type yeast
Campden tablets or strong sulphite
    solution

Activate the yeast starter bottle   Start records
Sterilise all equipment as required

Strip the elderberries from the stems, wash and crush them with the grapes. Add the washed minced sultanas, lemon juice and 3 pints of cold water and place in a plastic bucket. Add 1 crushed Campden tablet or 1 teaspoon strong sulphite solution and the pectin enzyme and leave covered for 24 hours. Add the active yeast starter and ferment on the pulp for 4 days, keeping the fruit submerged with a plate and the bucket tightly covered. Strain, dissolve the sugar in the must and pour into a demijohn. Add the grape concentrate and proceed as *in **Apple 1**.
    Mature in bulk for 18 months before bottling.

Weight	
4 lb	1.8 k
1 lb	453 g
½ lb	226 g
1 oz	30 g
1 teaspoon	5 g

Liquid measure	
1 gallon	4.5 l
1 pint	568 ml
½ pint	284 ml
1 fluid oz	28 ml
1 teaspoon	5 ml

Gooseberry 1

Sulphite for sterilising
Strong sulphite solution
Yeast starter bottle

2 lb gooseberries
1½ lb white sultanas
½ lb ripe bananas
1½ lb sugar
Water to 1 gallon

1 teaspoon pectin enzyme
1 teaspoon yeast nutrient
1 Vit B_1 tablet
Hock or Chablis type yeast
Campden tablets or strong sulphite
    solution

Activate the yeast starter bottle   Start records
Sterilise all equipment as required

Wash and crush the gooseberries, wash and mince the sultanas and place them
in a plastic bucket with 1 crushed Campden tablet or 1 teaspoon strong
sulphite solution, the pectin enzyme, yeast nutrient, Vit B_1 tablet and 5 pints
cold water. Boil the thinly sliced banana in ½ pint water for 20 minutes,
straining the liquid into the other ingredients. Leave covered for 24 hours
before adding the active yeast starter. Ferment on the pulp for 2 days, keeping
the fruit submerged with a plate and the bucket tightly covered. Strain and
pour the liquid into a demijohn, adding the dissolved sugar. Proceed as *in
Apple 1.
   Mature in bulk for 12 months before bottling.

Gooseberry 2

Sulphite for sterilising
Strong sulphite solution
Yeast starter bottle

2½ lb gooseberries
2 lb pears
½ lb ripe bananas
1¾ lb sugar
Water to 1 gallon

1 teaspoon pectin enzyme
1 teaspoon yeast nutrient
1 Vit B_1 tablet
Hock or Chablis type yeast
Campden tablets or strong sulphite
    solution

Activate the yeast starter bottle   Start records
Sterilise all equipment as required

Wash the gooseberries, crush or lightly liquidise them and place in a plastic
bucket with 5 pints of cold water and 1½ crushed Campden tablets or 1½
teaspoons strong sulphite solution. Wash and crush the pears and add them
with the pectin enzyme, yeast nutrient and Vit B_1 tablet. Boil the thinly sliced
bananas in 1 pint of water for 20 minutes and add the cooled strained liquid to
the other ingredients. Keep the fruit pulp submerged with a plate and leave for
3 days, stirring twice daily. Strain, pressing the pulp to extract as much liquid
as possible. Pour into a demijohn and add the yeast starter. Plug the top with
cotton wool and when the fermentation is active add the sugar syrup. Proceed
as *in **Apple 1**.
   Mature in bulk for 12 months before bottling.

Gooseberry 3

Sulphite for sterilising
Strong sulphite solution
Yeast starter bottle

2 lb gooseberries
1 large tin of apricots (1 lb 13 oz, 513 g)
1 lb white sultanas
½ pint mixed flower petals (rose, honeysuckle, pansy or broom)
1½ lb sugar
Water to 1 gallon

2 teaspoons pectin enzyme
1 teaspoon yeast nutrient
1 Vit B_1 tablet
Hock type yeast
Campden tablet or strong sulphite solution

**Activate the yeast starter bottle   Start records
Sterilise all equipment as required**

Wash and crush the gooseberries, wash, mince or lightly liquidise the sultanas and place them in a plastic bucket with 4 pints cold water, 1 crushed Campden tablet, the pectin enzyme, yeast nutrient and Vit B_1 tablet. Add the chopped apricots and juice and cover. Leave for 24 hours before adding the active yeast starter. When the fermentation is active add the crushed flowers and ferment on the pulp for 3 days, keeping the fruit pulp submerged with a plate and the bucket tightly covered. Strain, dissolve the sugar in the liquid and pour into a demijohn. Proceed as *in **Apple 1**.

The wine can be left with a little residual sugar if desired by racking when the S.G. drops to 1.000. Mature in bulk for 12 months before bottling and store for a further 6 months.

Gooseberry 4 (pasteurised)

Sulphite for sterilising
Strong sulphite solution
Yeast starter bottle

2 lb gooseberries
½ lb ripe bananas
1 pint white grape concentrate
1¼ lb sugar
Water to 1 gallon

2 teaspoons pectin enzyme
1 teaspoon yeast nutrient
1 Vit B_1 tablet
Hock type yeast
Campden tablets or strong sulphite solution

**Activate the yeast starter bottle   Start records
Sterilise all equipment as required**

Crush the gooseberries and place them in a stainless steel saucepan with 4 pints of cold water. Heat to 150°F (65°C), maintaining for 5 minutes. Strain, pressing the pulp lightly. Boil the thinly sliced bananas in 1 pint water for 20 minutes, strain the liquid and when cool add with the pectin enzyme, yeast nutrient and Vit B_1 tablet to the gooseberry juice. Pour into a demijohn adding the active yeast starter. When fermentation is active add the grape concentrate and dissolved sugar. Proceed as *in **Apple 1**.

Mature in bulk for 8 months before bottling.

Weight	
4 lb	1.8 k
1 lb	453 g
½ lb	226 g
1 oz	30 g
1 teaspoon	5 g

Liquid measure	
1 gallon	4.5 l
1 pint	568 ml
½ pint	284 ml
1 fluid oz	28 ml
1 teaspoon	5 ml

Loganberry 1

Sulphite for sterilising
Strong sulphite solution
Yeast starter bottle

1½ lb loganberries
1 lb redcurrants
1½ lb white sultanas
1½ lb sugar
Water to 1 gallon

1 teaspoon pectin enzyme
1 teaspoon yeast nutrient
1 Vit B_1 tablet
Bordeaux type yeast
Campden tablets or strong sulphite
    solution

**Activate the yeast starter bottle   Start records
Sterilise all equipment as required**

Crush the loganberries, strip the redcurrants from the stalks, crush and put
them in a plastic bucket with 5 pints of cold water. Wash and mince the
sultanas and add with 1 crushed Campden tablet or 1 teaspoon strong sulphite
solution, the pectin enzyme, yeast nutrient and Vit B_1 tablet. Stir, cover and
leave for 24 hours. Add the active yeast starter and ferment on the pulp for 3
days, keeping the fruit submerged with a plate and the bucket tightly covered.
Strain and pour into a demijohn with the dissolved sugar. Proceed as *in
Apple 1.

Mature for 12 months in bulk before bottling.

Loganberry 2

Sulphite for sterilising
Strong sulphite solution
Yeast starter bottle

2 lb loganberries
2 lb pears
¾ pint red grape concentrate
1½ lb sugar
Water to 1 gallon

1 teaspoon pectin enzyme
1 teaspoon yeast nutrient
1 Vit B_1 tablet
Bordeaux type yeast
Campden tablets or strong sulphite
    solution

**Activate the yeast starter bottle   Start records
Sterilise all equipment as required**

Crush the loganberries and place them in a plastic bucket with 4 pints of cold
water and 1 crushed Campden tablet or 1 teaspoon strong sulphite solution.
Wash and crush the pears and add with the pectin enzyme, yeast nutrient and
Vit B_1 tablet. Stir, cover and leave for 24 hours before adding the active yeast
starter. Ferment on the pulp for 3 days, keeping the fruit submerged with a
plate and the bucket tightly covered. Strain and pour into a demijohn with the
grape concentrate and the dissolved sugar. Proceed as *in **Apple 1**.

The wine can be left with a little residual sugar if desired by racking when
the S.G. drops to 1.000. Mature in bulk for 8 months before bottling.

Orange 1

Sulphite for sterilising
Strong sulphite solution
Yeast starter bottle

10 medium sized oranges
1 lb white sultanas
2 lb sugar
Water to 1 gallon

2 teaspoons pectin enzyme
1 teaspoon yeast nutrient
1 Vit B_1 tablet
All-purpose wine yeast
Campden tablets or strong sulphite
    solution

Activate the yeast starter bottle   **Start records**
Sterilise all equipment as required

Squeeze the juice from the oranges, strain and pour into a plastic bucket with 2 pints of water. Finely grate or thinly pare the peel from a few of the oranges, avoiding the white pith (about 2 oz is adequate) and pour 2 pints of boiling water over the peel. Leave to cool and add to the orange juice with the washed minced sultanas, pectin enzyme, yeast nutrient, Vit B_1 tablet and active yeast starter. Ferment on the pulp for 2 days, keeping the fruit submerged and the bucket tightly covered. Strain, pressing the pulp, and pour into a demijohn with the dissolved sugar. Proceed as *in **Apple 1**.

   Mature in bulk for 6 months before bottling.

Orange 2

Sulphite for sterilising
Strong sulphite solution
Yeast starter bottle

1 litre carton pure orange juice
2 lb apples
1 lb pears
1 lb sultanas
1½ lb sugar
Water to 1 gallon

2 teaspoons pectin enzyme
1 teaspoon yeast nutrient
1 Vit B_1 tablet
Bordeaux type yeast
Campden tablets or strong sulphite
    solution

Activate the yeast starter bottle   **Start records**
Sterilise all equipment as required

Wash the apples and pears, crush or finely chop them and place in a bucket with 3 pints of cold water, 1 crushed Campden tablet or 1 teaspoon strong sulphite solution and the orange juice. Wash and mince or lightly liquidise the sultanas and add with the pectin enzyme, yeast nutrient and Vit B_1 tablet. Stir and leave for 24 hours keeping the fruit submerged. Add the active yeast starter and ferment on the pulp for 3 days, still keeping the fruit submerged and the bucket tightly covered. Strain, pressing the pulp, and pour into a demijohn. Add the dissolved sugar and proceed as *in **Apple 1**.

   Mature in bulk for 8 months before bottling.

Weight	
4 lb	1.8 k
1 lb	453 g
½ lb	226 g
1 oz	30 g
1 teaspoon	5 g

Liquid measure	
1 gallon	4.5 l
1 pint	568 ml
½ pint	284 ml
1 fluid oz	28 ml
1 teaspoon	5 ml

P ear 1

Sulphite for sterilising
Strong sulphite solution
Yeast starter bottle

3 lb pears
1 lb gooseberries
1 lb white sultanas
1¾ lb sugar
Water to 1 gallon

1 teaspoon pectin enzyme
1 teaspoon yeast nutrient
1 Vit B_1 tablet
Hock or Chablis type yeast
Campden tablets or strong sulphite
solution

Activate the yeast starter bottle   **Start records**
Sterilise all equipment as required

Wash and crush the pears and gooseberries, wash and mince the sultanas and
place them in a plastic bucket with 4 pints of cold water, 1 crushed Campden
tablet or 1 teaspoon strong sulphite solution, the pectin enzyme, yeast nutrient
and Vit B_1 tablet. Stir well, keep the fruit submerged with a plate and leave for
24 hours. Add the active yeast starter and ferment on the pulp for 3 days, still
keeping the fruit submerged and the bucket tightly covered. Strain, pressing
the pulp, and pour into a demijohn. Add the dissolved sugar and proceed as
*in **Apple 1**.

Mature in bulk for 8 months before bottling.

P ear 2

Sulphite for sterilising
Strong sulphite solution
Yeast starter bottle

2 lb pears
1½ lb white sultanas
2 small bottles pineapple juice (e.g. Britvic)
1½ lb sugar
Water to 1 gallon

1 teaspoon pectin enzyme
1 teaspoon yeast nutrient
1 Vit B_1 tablet
Hock type yeast
Campden tablets or strong sulphite
solution

Activate the yeast starter bottle   **Start records**
Sterilise all equipment as required

Wash and crush the pears and place them in a plastic bucket with 4 pints of
cold water and 1 crushed Campden tablet or 1 teaspoon strong sulphite
solution. Wash and mince the sultanas and add with the pectin enzyme, yeast
nutrient, Vit B_1 tablet and the pineapple juice. Stir well, keep the fruit
submerged with a plate and leave for 24 hours. Add the active yeast starter and
ferment on the pulp for 3 days. Strain and pour into a demijohn, adding the
dissolved sugar. Proceed as *in **Apple 1**.

Mature in bulk for 6 months before bottling. The wine may be sweetened if
desired.

Pear and plum

Sulphite for sterilising
Strong sulphite solution
Yeast starter bottle

2 lb pears
2 lb Golden Egg plums
½ lb white sultanas
½ lb ripe bananas
2 fl oz lemon juice
1¾ lb sugar
Water to 1 gallon

1 teaspoon pectin enzyme
1 teaspoon yeast nutrient
1 Vit B_1 tablet
Bordeaux type yeast
Campden tablets or strong sulphite
  solution

**Activate the yeast starter bottle   Start records
Sterilise all equipment as required**

Wash and stone the plums and crush in 5 pints of cold water, adding 1 crushed
Campden tablet or 1 teaspoon strong sulphite solution. Wash the pears, crush
and add them, together with the washed minced sultanas, lemon juice and the
liquid from ½ lb boiled bananas, the pectin enzyme, yeast nutrient and Vit B_1
tablet. Stir well, submerge the fruit pulp and leave for 24 hours before adding
the active yeast starter. Ferment on the pulp for 3 days, still keeping the fruit
submerged and the bucket tightly covered. Strain carefully, add the dissolved
sugar syrup and pour into a demijohn. Proceed as *in **Apple 1**.
    Mature in bulk for 12 months before bottling.

Pineapple 1

Sulphite for sterilising
Strong sulphite solution
Yeast starter bottle

1 medium sized fresh pineapple
1½ lb white sultanas
3 ripe bananas
1¼ lb sugar
Water to 1 gallon

1 teaspoon pectin enzyme
1 teaspoon yeast nutrient
1 Vit B_1 tablet
Sauternes type yeast
Campden tablets or strong sulphite
  solution

**Activate the yeast starter bottle   Start records
Sterilise all equipment as required**

Select a fully ripened pineapple (the skin should be a deep orange and pliable to
the touch), wash thoroughly and remove the top and the hard core at the
bottom. Slice into small pieces and add 4 pints of cold water, 1 crushed
Campden tablet or 1 teaspoon strong sulphite solution. Wash the sultanas,
mince and add. Slice the bananas thinly and boil in 1 pint of water for 20
minutes; add the strained liquid. When cool add the pectin enzyme, yeast
nutrient and Vit B_1 tablet. Stir well and leave for 24 hours, keeping the fruit
submerged. Add the active yeast starter and ferment on the pulp for 3 days,
still keeping the fruit submerged and the bucket tightly covered. Strain and
pour into a demijohn, adding the dissolved sugar. Proceed as *in **Apple 1**.
    Rack when the S.G. reaches 1.000 and mature for 12 months before bottling.

Weight	
4 lb	1.8 k
1 lb	453 g
½ lb	226 g
1 oz	30 g
1 teaspoon	5 g

Liquid measure	
1 gallon	4.5 l
1 pint	568 ml
½ pint	284 ml
1 fluid oz	28 ml
1 teaspoon	5 ml

Pineapple 2

Sulphite for sterilising
Strong sulphite solution
Yeast starter bottle

1 large tin pineapple juice (1.19 l)
1½ lb white sultanas
1 lb ripe bananas
1¼ lb sugar
Water to 1 gallon

1 teaspoon pectin enzyme
1 teaspoon yeast nutrient
1 Vit B_1 tablet
Bordeaux type yeast
Campden tablet or strong sulphite
    solution

Activate the yeast starter bottle   **Start records**
Sterilise all equipment as required

Wash the sultanas thoroughly, mince or lightly liquidise them in 4 pints of cold water and place in a plastic bucket. Slice the bananas thinly and boil in 1 pint of water for 20 minutes; add the strained liquid to the sultanas, the pineapple juice, ½ crushed Campden tablet or ½ teaspoon strong sulphite solution, the pectin enzyme, yeast nutrient and Vit B_1 tablet. Stir well, cover and leave for 24 hours before adding the active yeast starter. Ferment on the pulp for 3 days, keeping the fruit submerged with a plate and the bucket tightly covered. Strain and pour into a demijohn with the dissolved sugar. Proceed as *in **Apple 1**.

    Mature in bulk for 8 months before bottling. The wine can be left with a little residual sugar if desired by racking when the S.G. drops to 1.000.

Raspberry 1

Sulphite for sterilising
Strong sulphite solution
Yeast starter bottle

2 lb raspberries
1 lb redcurrants
1 lb sultanas
½ lb ripe bananas
1½ lb sugar
Water to 1 gallon

1 teaspoon pectin enzyme
1 teaspoon yeast nutrient
1 Vit B_1 tablet
Burgundy or Bordeaux type yeast
Campden tablet or strong sulphite
    solution

Activate the yeast starter bottle   **Start records**
Sterilise all equipment as required

Carefully check the raspberries, discarding any with mould, and place them in a plastic bucket; strip the redcurrants from their stalks and place with the raspberries, crush the fruit thoroughly, add the washed minced sultanas, the thinly sliced bananas and 5 pints of cold water, 1 crushed Campden tablet or 1 teaspoon strong sulphite solution, the pectin enzyme, yeast nutrient and Vit B_1 tablet. Stir well, cover and leave for 24 hours. Add the active yeast starter and ferment on the pulp for 2 days. Strain and pour into a demijohn with the dissolved sugar. Proceed as *in **Apple 1**.

    The wine may be racked when the S.G. drops to 1.000, leaving a little residual sugar. Store 12 months before bottling.

Raspberry 2

Sulphite for sterilising
Strong sulphite solution
Yeast starter bottle

2 lb raspberries
1 lb ripe bananas
1 pint red grape concentrate
1½ lb sugar
Water to 1 gallon

1 teaspoon pectin enzyme
1 teaspoon yeast nutrient
1 Vit B_1 tablet
Burgundy or Bordeaux type yeast
Campden tablet or strong sulphite
  solution

Activate the yeast starter bottle   Start records
Sterilise all equipment as required

Carefully check the raspberries, discarding any that are mouldy, and crush them in a plastic bucket with 4 pints of cold water. Slice the bananas thinly and boil in 1 pint of water for 20 minutes. Strain the liquid into the crushed raspberries and when cool add 1 crushed Campden tablet or 1 teaspoon strong sulphite solution, the pectin enzyme, yeast nutrient and Vit B_1 tablet. Stir well and leave for 24 hours. Strain the liquid, pressing the pulp, and add the active yeast starter. Pour into a demijohn, plugging the top with cotton wool. When the fermentation is active add the grape concentrate and the dissolved sugar. Proceed as *in **Apple 1**.

  Mature in bulk for 8 months before bottling. The wine may be racked when the S.G. drops to 1.000, leaving a little residual sugar.

Raspberry 3 (pasteurised)

Sulphite for sterilising
Strong sulphite solution
Yeast starter bottle

2 lb raspberries
1 lb black or redcurrants
¾ pint red grape concentrate
1½ lb sugar
Water to 1 gallon

2 teaspoons pectin enzyme
1 teaspoon yeast nutrient
1 Vit B_1 tablet
Burgundy or Bordeaux type yeast
Campden tablets or strong sulphite
  solution

Activate the yeast starter bottle   Start records
Sterilise all equipment as required

Crush the raspberries and currants and place in a stainless steel saucepan with 4 pints of cold water. Heat to 150°F (65°C), maintaining this heat for 5 minutes. Remove from the heat and cool. Strain, pressing the pulp lightly. Add the pectin enzyme, yeast nutrient, Vit B_1 tablet and the active yeast starter and pour into a demijohn, plugging the top with cotton wool. When the fermentation is active add the grape concentrate and the dissolved sugar. Proceed as *in **Apple 1**.

  The wine should be matured in bulk for 8 months before bottling and can be left with a little residual sugar.

Note: Over-ripe fruit can be used in this recipe, or fruits that have been picked the previous day and not processed.

Weight	
4 lb	1.8 k
1 lb	453 g
½ lb	226 g
1 oz	30 g
1 teaspoon	5 g

Liquid measure	
1 gallon	4.5 l
1 pint	568 ml
½ pint	284 ml
1 fluid oz	28 ml
1 teaspoon	5 ml

Rosehip

Sulphite for sterilising
Strong sulphite solution
Yeast starter bottle

2 lb rosehips
2 lb apples
2 lb pears
4 oz dried figs
1¾ lb sugar
Water to 1 gallon

1 teaspoon pectin enzyme
1 teaspoon yeast nutrient
1 Vit B_1 tablet
All-purpose yeast starter
Campden tablets or strong sulphite
 solution

Activate the yeast starter bottle   **Start records**
Sterilise all equipment as required

Place the rosehips in a stainless steel saucepan with 5 pints of cold water, heat to 150°F (65°C) and maintain for 15 minutes. Remove from the heat and leave to cool. Crush the softened rosehips and add 1 crushed Campden tablet or 1 teaspoon strong sulphite solution and place in a plastic bucket. Wash the apples and pears, chop or crush them and place in the bucket. Wash the figs and slice them thinly; add with the pectin enzyme, yeast nutrient and Vit B_1 tablet. Stir well, keep the fruit submerged with an upturned plate and the bucket tightly covered. After 24 hours add the active yeast starter and ferment on the pulp for 3 days. Strain the liquid into a demijohn and add the dissolved sugar. Proceed as *in **Apple 1**.

  Mature in bulk for 6 months before bottling.

Rhubarb

Sulphite for sterilising
Strong sulphite solution
Yeast starter bottle

3 lb rhubarb
1 lb white sultanas
1 lb ripe bananas
4 oranges
1½ lb sugar
Water to 1 gallon

1 teaspoon pectin enzyme
1 teaspoon yeast nutrient
1 Vit B_1 tablet
All-purpose yeast starter
Campden tablets or strong sulphite
 solution

Activate the yeast starter bottle   **Start records**
Sterilise all equipment as required

Use only young stalks of rhubarb. Trim off the white base and the green leaf and wash the sticks. Chop very finely or chop and liquidise in 5 pints of cold water. Place in a plastic bucket with 1 crushed Campden tablet or 1 teaspoon strong sulphite solution and the pectin enzyme. Keep the fruit submerged with an upturned plate and leave for 48 hours, stirring two or three times daily. Strain off the liquid and return it to the bucket. Slice the bananas thinly and boil for 20 minutes in 1 pint of water; strain the liquid into the rhubarb juice. Add the washed minced sultanas, the juice from the oranges, yeast nutrient, Vit B_1 tablet and the active yeast starter. Ferment on the pulp for 3 days. Strain and pour into a demijohn with the dissolved sugar. Proceed as *in **Apple 1**.

  Mature in bulk for 8 months before bottling.

Sloe 1 (pasteurised)

Sulphite for sterilising
Strong sulphite solution
Yeast starter bottle

2 lb sloes
1 lb ripe bananas
¾ pint red grape concentrate
1¼ lb sugar
Water to 1 gallon

1 teaspoon pectin enzyme
1 teaspoon yeast nutrient
1 Vit B_1 tablet
Bordeaux type yeast
Campden tablets or strong sulphite
   solution

Activate the yeast starter bottle   Start records
Sterilise all equipment as required

Crush the sloes just enough to break the skins and place in a stainless steel
saucepan with 4 pints of cold water. Heat to 150°F (65°C), maintaining this
heat for 5 minutes. Remove and leave to cool. Thinly slice the bananas and boil
for 20 minutes in 1 pint of water, then strain the liquid into the sloes. When
cool add the pectin enzyme and leave covered for 24 hours. Strain, pressing the
pulp, and add the yeast nutrient, Vit B_1 tablet and active yeast starter. Pour into
a demijohn and plug the top with cotton wool. When the fermentation is active
add the grape concentrate and dissolved sugar. Proceed as *in **Apple 1**.

   Mature in bulk for 8 months before bottling.

Sloe 2

Sulphite for sterilising
Strong sulphite solution
Yeast starter bottle

2 lb ripe sloes
1 lb jar bilberries
½ lb dried currants
1 lb sultanas
1½ lb sugar
Water to 1 gallon

1 teaspoon pectin enzyme
1 teaspoon yeast nutrient
1 Vit B_1 tablet
Bordeaux type yeast
Campden tablets or strong sulphite
   solution

Activate the yeast starter bottle   Start records
Sterilise all equipment as required

Wash and crush the sloes, taking care not to break the stones. Wash and mince
or lightly liquidise the currants and sultanas and place them in a plastic bucket
with 5 pints of cold water. Add 1 crushed Campden tablet or 1 teaspoon strong
sulphite solution, the pectin enzyme, yeast nutrient and Vit B_1 tablet. Stir well
and leave for 24 hours. Add the jar of bilberries and the active yeast starter and
ferment on the pulp for 4 days, keeping the fruit submerged and the bucket
tightly covered. Strain and pour into a demijohn with the dissolved sugar.
Proceed as *in **Apple 1**.

   Mature in bulk for 18 months before bottling.

Weight	
4 lb	1.8 k
1 lb	453 g
½ lb	226 g
1 oz	30 g
1 teaspoon	5 g
Liquid measure	
1 gallon	4.5 l
1 pint	568 ml
½ pint	284 ml
1 fluid oz	28 ml
1 teaspoon	5 ml

Strawberry 1

Sulphite for sterilising
Strong sulphite solution
Yeast starter bottle

2 lb strawberries
½ lb blackcurrants
1 lb sultanas
2 ripe bananas
1½ lb sugar
Water to 1 gallon

1 teaspoon pectin enzyme
1 teaspoon yeast nutrient
1 Vit B₁ tablet
Burgundy or Bordeaux type yeast
Campden tablet or strong sulphite
  solution

Activate the yeast starter bottle   **Start records**
Sterilise all equipment as required

Crush the strawberries, wash and crush the blackcurrants, wash and mince the sultanas and thinly slice the bananas. Place in a plastic bucket with 5 pints of cold water, 1 crushed Campden tablet or 1 teaspoon strong sulphite solution, the pectin enzyme, yeast nutrient and Vit B₁ tablet. Stir, keep the fruit submerged with a plate and the bucket tightly covered. Leave for 24 hours before adding the active yeast starter. Ferment on the pulp for 3 days, always keeping the fruit submerged. Strain, pressing the pulp lightly, and pour into a demijohn with the dissolved sugar. Proceed as *in **Apple 1**.

Mature in bulk for 8 months before bottling. The wine may be racked when the S.G. drops to 1.000, leaving a little residual sugar.

Strawberry 2

Sulphite for sterilising
Strong sulphite solution
Yeast starter bottle

2 lb strawberries
¾ lb gooseberries or redcurrants
2 ripe bananas
¾ pint red grape concentrate
1¼ lb sugar
Water to 1 gallon

1 teaspoon pectin enzyme
1 teaspoon yeast nutrient
1 Vit B$_1$ tablet
Burgundy or Bordeaux type yeast
Campden tablets or strong sulphite
  solution

Activate the yeast starter bottle   Start records
Sterilise all equipment as required

Crush the strawberries, wash and crush the gooseberries or redcurrants, thinly
slice the bananas and place in a plastic bucket with 4 pints of cold water, 1
crushed Campden tablet or 1 teaspoon strong sulphite solution, the pectin
enzyme, yeast nutrient and Vit B$_1$ tablet. Stir well, keep the fruit submerged
with a plate and the bucket covered. Leave 24 hours before adding the active
yeast starter and ferment on the pulp for 3 days. Strain, pour into a demijohn
and add the grape concentrate and dissolved sugar. Proceed as *in **Apple 1**.

Mature in bulk for 12 months before bottling. The wine may be racked
when the S.G. reaches 1.000, leaving a little residual sugar.

Weight	
4 lb	1.8 k
1 lb	453 g
½ lb	226 g
1 oz	30 g
1 teaspoon	5 g
Liquid measure	
1 gallon	4.5 l
1 pint	568 ml
½ pint	284 ml
1 fluid oz	28 ml
1 teaspoon	5 ml

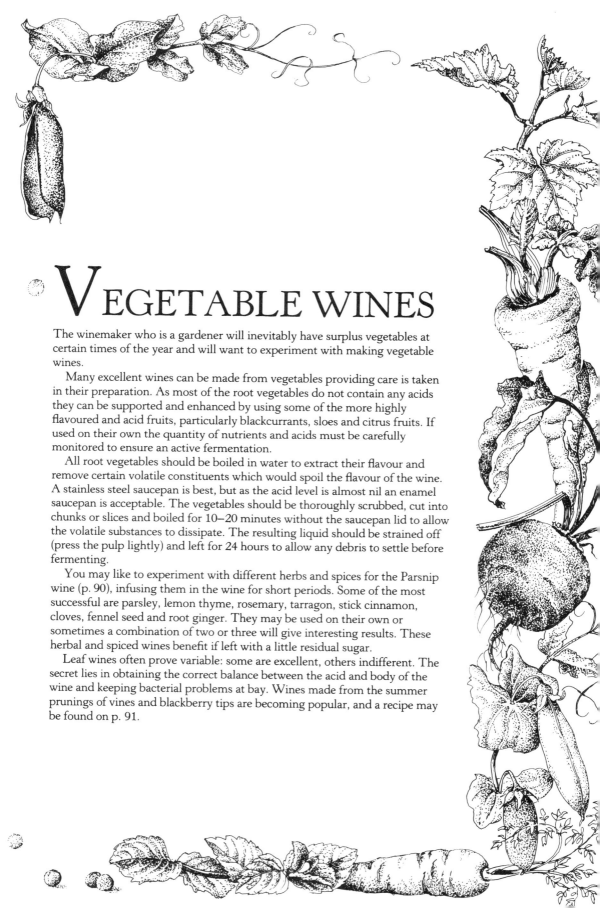

VEGETABLE WINES

The winemaker who is a gardener will inevitably have surplus vegetables at certain times of the year and will want to experiment with making vegetable wines.

Many excellent wines can be made from vegetables providing care is taken in their preparation. As most of the root vegetables do not contain any acids they can be supported and enhanced by using some of the more highly flavoured and acid fruits, particularly blackcurrants, sloes and citrus fruits. If used on their own the quantity of nutrients and acids must be carefully monitored to ensure an active fermentation.

All root vegetables should be boiled in water to extract their flavour and remove certain volatile constituents which would spoil the flavour of the wine. A stainless steel saucepan is best, but as the acid level is almost nil an enamel saucepan is acceptable. The vegetables should be thoroughly scrubbed, cut into chunks or slices and boiled for 10–20 minutes without the saucepan lid to allow the volatile substances to dissipate. The resulting liquid should be strained off (press the pulp lightly) and left for 24 hours to allow any debris to settle before fermenting.

You may like to experiment with different herbs and spices for the Parsnip wine (p. 90), infusing them in the wine for short periods. Some of the most successful are parsley, lemon thyme, rosemary, tarragon, stick cinnamon, cloves, fennel seed and root ginger. They may be used on their own or sometimes a combination of two or three will give interesting results. These herbal and spiced wines benefit if left with a little residual sugar.

Leaf wines often prove variable: some are excellent, others indifferent. The secret lies in obtaining the correct balance between the acid and body of the wine and keeping bacterial problems at bay. Wines made from the summer prunings of vines and blackberry tips are becoming popular, and a recipe may be found on p. 91.

Beetroot 1

Sulphite for sterilising   *Dissolve 8 Campden tablets or ½ oz sodium or potassium metabisulphite in 2 pints of water and store in a screw-topped bottle.*
Strong sulphite solution   *Add 1 oz sodium or potassium metabisulphite to ½ pint water. Store in a small screw-topped bottle.*
Yeast starter bottle   *Sterilise a small bottle either by boiling for 20 minutes or filling with sterilising sulphite and leaving for 20 minutes. Pour back into the storage bottle and rinse twice to remove any sulphite solution. Half fill the bottle with cool boiled water, add the juice from half a lemon, 2 teaspoons granulated sugar and the wine yeast. Shake the bottle, plug with cotton wool and leave in a warm place of 65–70°F (18–21°C) for 48 hours.*

4 lb beetroots	Water to 1 gallon
1 lb blackcurrants or ½ lb blackberries and	1 teaspoon pectin enzyme
½ lb sloes	1 teaspoon yeast nutrient
½ lb dried currants	1 Vit B₁ tablet
½ lb sultanas	Burgundy type yeast
¼ oz malic acid	Campden tablets or strong sulphite
2 lb sugar	solution

Activate the yeast starter bottle   Start records
Sterilise all equipment as required   *Prepare the covered plastic bucket and utensils by washing thoroughly with warm water. Place the utensils to be used in the bucket: pour in the sterilising solution. Replace lid tightly and swirl the solution around, making sure that it reaches all parts of the bucket. Leave for 20 minutes (longer if possible) before returning the solution to the storage bottle. It will remain effective for quite a long while providing it retains its pungent odour. Carefully wash the bucket and utensils with tap water to remove all traces of sulphite before use.*

Wash the blackcurrants (or blackberries and sloes), the dried currants and sultanas, lightly liquidise or crush them and place in a fermentation bucket with 3 pints cold water. Add 1 crushed Campden tablet or 1 teaspoon strong sulphite solution, the pectin enzyme, malic acid, yeast nutrient and Vit B₁ tablet and cover.

   Wash and scrub the beetroots and slice them; cover with 7 pints of cold water and bring to the boil. Boil for 30 minutes without the lid. Strain the liquid from the pulp and leave it to settle. After 24 hours syphon the clear liquid from the sediment into the other ingredients in the bucket. Stir, and add the active yeast starter, pouring it carefully into the fruit pulp at one side to enable a colony to become established. Cover the bucket tightly. When the yeast activity is obvious stir it into the bulk and ferment on the pulp for 3 days, keeping the cap submerged with a plate. Strain and pour into a demijohn adding the dissolved sugar.

The jar should be no more than seven-eighths full. Fit an airlock and leave in a warm place to ferment. Top up after a couple of days with a little cold water. When the fermentation ceases syphon the clearing wine from the lees (sediment) into a clean jar and move to a cool place. After one or two days rack again, adding 2 Campden tablets or 2 teaspoons strong sulphite solution. Top up with a litttle cold water. Rack again after 2 weeks, adding 2 more Campden tablets or 2 teaspoons strong sulphite solution. Top up again and replace the airlock with a cork bung. Store in a cool place.

The wine should be racked again when necessary and matured in bulk for at least 18 months before bottling, then stored in bottle for another six.

Weight	
4 lb	1.8 k
1 lb	453 g
½ lb	226 g
1 oz	30 g
1 teaspoon	5 g

Liquid measure	
1 gallon	4.5 l
1 pint	568 ml
½ pint	284 ml
1 fluid oz	28 ml
1 teaspoon	5 ml

Beetroot 2

Sulphite for sterilising
Strong sulphite solution
Yeast starter bottle

4 lb beetroots
¾ pint red grape concentrate
½ oz tartaric acid
¼ oz malic acid
¼ teaspoon grape tannin
2 lb sugar
Water to 1 gallon

1 teaspoon pectin enzyme
1 teaspoon yeast nutrient
2 Vit B₁ tablets
Burgundy type yeast
Campden tablets or strong sulphite
    solution

Activate the yeast starter bottle   **Start records**
Sterilise all equipment as required

Wash and scrub the beetroots, slice them and cover with 7 pints of cold water;
bring to the boil. Boil for 30 minutes without the lid. Strain from the pulp and
leave to settle. After 24 hours syphon the clear liquid from the sediment, add
the red grape concentrate, tartaric and malic acids, grape tannin, pectin
enzyme, yeast nutrient and Vit B₁ tablet. Stir until the ingredients are dissolved
and pour into a demijohn, adding the active yeast starter. Plug the top with
cotton wool. When the fermentation is active add the dissolved sugar and fit an
airlock. Proceed as *in **Beetroot 1**.

Mature in bulk for 12 months before bottling.

Carrot 1

Sulphite for sterilising
Strong sulphite solution
Yeast starter bottle

3 lb carrots
1 lb bananas
4 oranges
2 fl oz lemon juice
½ oz tartaric acid
½ teaspoon grape tannin
2 lb sugar
Water to 1 gallon

1 teaspoon pectin enzyme
1 teaspoon yeast nutrient
2 Vit B₁ tablets
Bordeaux type yeast
Campden tablets or strong sulphite
    solution

Activate the yeast starter bottle   **Start records**
Sterilise all equipment as required

Wash and scrub the carrots, slice them thinly and place in a saucepan with 7
pints of cold water. Skin the bananas, slice finely and add with a little grated
peel from 2 oranges. Boil for 30 minutes without the lid. Strain from the pulp
and leave to settle. After 24 hours syphon the clear liquid from the sediment,
add the orange and lemon juice, tartaric acid, grape tannin, pectin enzyme,
yeast nutrient and Vit B₁ tablets. Stir well until the ingredients are dissolved
and pour into the demijohn, adding the active yeast starter. Plug the top with
cotton wool. When the fermentation is active add the dissolved sugar and fit an
airlock. Proceed as *in **Beetroot 1**.

Mature in bulk for 15 months before bottling.

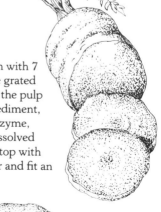

Carrot 2

Sulphite for sterilising
Strong sulphite solution
Yeast starter bottle

3 lb carrots
1½ lb muscatel raisins
½ oz tartaric acid
¼ oz malic acid
½ teaspoon grape tannin
1¾ lb sugar
Water to 1 gallon

1 teaspoon pectin enzyme
1 teaspoon yeast nutrient
1 Vit B_1 tablet
Bordeaux type yeast
Campden tablets or strong sulphite
    solution

Activate the yeast starter bottle   **Start records**
Sterilise all equipment as required

Wash and scrub the carrots, slice them thinly and place in a saucepan with 7 pints of cold water. Boil without the lid for 30 minutes. Strain from the pulp and leave to settle. After 24 hours syphon the clear liquid from the sediment. Wash the raisins and mince or lightly liquidise them in the liquid, place in a plastic bucket with the tartaric and malic acids, grape tannin, pectin enzyme, yeast nutrient, Vit B_1 tablet and the active yeast starter. Cover and ferment on the pulp for 3 days, keeping the fruit submerged and the bucket tightly covered. Strain, pour into the demijohn with the dissolved sugar and fit an airlock. Proceed as *in **Beetroot 1**.

    Mature in bulk for 15 months before bottling.

Parsnip 1

Sulphite for sterilising
Strong sulphite solution
Yeast starter bottle

4 lb parsnips
1 tin pineapple juice (18.5 fl oz, 525 ml)
½ lb sultanas
½ lb ripe bananas
¼ oz malic acid
¼ oz tartaric acid
½ teaspoon grape tannin
2 lb sugar
Water to 1 gallon

1 teaspoon pectin enzyme
1 teaspoon yeast nutrient
1 Vit B_1 tablet
Bordeaux type yeast
Campden tablets or strong sulphite
    solution

Activate the yeast starter bottle   **Start records**
Sterilise all equipment as required

Wash and scrub the parsnips, slice them thinly and place in a saucepan with 7 pints of cold water. Skin the bananas, slice and add. Boil for 30 minutes without the lid. Strain from the pulp and leave to settle. After 24 hours syphon the clear liquid from the sediment. Wash and mince the sultanas and add with the pineapple juice, tartaric and malic acids, grape tannin, pectin enzyme, yeast nutrient, Vit B_1 tablet. Stir well and add the yeast starter. Ferment on the pulp for 24 hours before straining and pouring into a demijohn with the dissolved sugar. Fit an airlock and proceed as *in **Beetroot 1**.

    Mature in bulk for 15–18 months before bottling.

Weight	
4 lb	1.8 k
1 lb	453 g
½ lb	226 g
1 oz	30 g
1 teaspoon	5 g

Liquid measure	
1 gallon	4.5 l
1 pint	568 ml
½ pint	284 ml
1 fluid oz	28 ml
1 teaspoon	5 ml

Parsnip 2

Sulphite for sterilising
Strong sulphite solution
Yeast starter bottle

4 lb parsnips
1 lb ripe bananas
¾ pint grape concentrate (white)
¼ pint elderflowers or rose petals
½ oz tartaric acid
½ teaspoon grape tannin
1¾ lb sugar

Water to 1 gallon
1 teaspoon pectin enzyme
1 teaspoon yeast nutrient
1 Vit B_1 tablet
Sauternes type yeast
Campden tablets or strong sulphite
  solution

Activate the yeast starter bottle   **Start records**
Sterilise all equipment as required

Wash and scrub the parsnips, slice them thinly or cut into chunks, skin and slice the bananas and place all in a saucepan with 6 pints of cold water. Boil for 30 minutes. Strain from the pulp and leave to settle. After 24 hours syphon the clear liquid from the sediment. Add the grape concentrate, tartaric acid, grape tannin, pectin enzyme, yeast nutrient, Vit B_1 tablet. Stir and pour into a demijohn. Add the active yeast starter and plug the top of the jar with cotton wool. When the fermentation is active add the dissolved sugar and drop in the crushed flower petals. Fit an airlock and ferment for 1 week before straining off the flower petals. Return the must to the demijohn to complete fermentation. Proceed as *in **Beetroot 1**.

Mature in bulk for 12 months before bottling. The wine is improved if left with a little residual sugar.

Parsnip with herbs

Sulphite for sterilising
Strong sulphite solution
Yeast starter bottle

4 lb parsnips
1 lb ripe bananas
2 pints apple juice
¾ oz tartaric acid
½ teaspoon grape tannin
½ tea-cup mint leaves
1 teaspoon carraway seeds
2 lb sugar

Water to 1 gallon
1 teaspoon pectin enzyme
1 teaspoon yeast nutrient
1 Vit B_1 tablet
All-purpose wine yeast
Campden tablets or strong sulphite
  solution

Activate the yeast starter bottle   **Start records**
Sterilise all equipment as required

Wash and scrub the parsnips and cut them into small chunks. Skin the bananas, slice them and place in a saucepan with 6 pints of cold water. Boil for 30 minutes. Strain from the pulp and leave to settle. After 24 hours syphon the clear liquid from the sediment. Add the apple juice, tartaric acid, grape tannin, pectin enzyme, yeast nutrient and Vit B_1 tablet. Stir and pour into a demijohn with the active yeast starter. Plug the top with cotton wool. When the fermentation is active add the dissolved sugar and fit an airlock. After the first vigorous fermentation pick the mint, crush it and put with the carraway seeds in a small piece of nylon or muslin. Tie this with a piece of cotton, leaving long ends to suspend the bag in the wine. Each day remove the airlock and give the cotton attachment a few jerks to distribute the flavour. After 5 days, or when enough flavour for your taste has been extracted, take out the sachet and proceed as *in **Beetroot 1**.

Mature in bulk for at least 12 months before bottling.

Pea pod wine

Sulphite for sterilising
Strong sulphite solution
Yeast starter bottle

4 lb pea pods
1 lb ripe bananas
6 fl oz lemon juice
¼ oz malic acid
½ teaspoon grape tannin
2 lb sugar
Water to 1 gallon

1 teaspoon pectin enzyme
1 teaspoon yeast nutrient
1 Vit B_1 tablet
All-purpose type yeast
Campden tablets or strong sulphite
    solution

Activate the yeast starter bottle   **Start records**
Sterilise all equipment as required

Wash the pea pods, chop them and place in a large saucepan with the thinly
sliced bananas and 7 pints of cold water. Bring to the boil and boil for 20
minutes. Strain from the pulp and leave to settle. After 24 hours syphon the
clear liquid from the sediment. Add the lemon juice, malic acid, grape tannin,
pectin enzyme, yeast nutrient and Vit B_1 tablet. Stir until the ingredients have
dissolved and pour into a demijohn, adding the yeast starter. Plug the top with
cotton wool. When the fermentation is active add the dissolved sugar and fit an
airlock. Proceed as *in **Beetroot 1**.

   Mature in bulk for 8 months before bottling.

Folly or bramble tip wine

Sulphite for sterilising
Strong sulphite solution
Yeast starter bottle

Very successful wines can be made from the young shoots and leaves from
vines. These can be gathered during summer pruning; it is important to select
only the young leaves and shoots and not mature leaves. Alternatively bramble
tips may be used.

5 lb vine or bramble shoots or leaves
1 lb ripe bananas
¾ pint grape concentrate
¼ oz tartaric acid
¼ oz malic acid
½ teaspoon grape tannin
1¾ lb sugar
Water to 1 gallon

1 teaspoon pectin enzyme
1 teaspoon yeast nutrient
1 Vit B_1 tablet
Hock type yeast
Campden tablets or strong sulphite
    solution

Activate the yeast starter bottle   **Start records**
Sterilise all equipment as required

Break the leaves into small pieces and place in a preserving pan. Pour over
them 6 pints of boiling water, stir several times and leave for 24 hours. Strain,
pressing the leaves. Thinly slice the bananas and boil in 1 pint of water for 20
minutes; add the strained liquid, the tartaric acid, malic acid, grape tannin,
grape concentrate, pectin enzyme, yeast nutrient and Vit B_1 tablet. Stir well
until all the ingredients have dissolved and pour into a demijohn. Add the yeast
starter and plug the top of the demijohn with cotton wool. When the
fermentation is active add the dissolved sugar and fit an airlock. Proceed as *in
Beetroot 1.

   Mature in bulk for 8 months before bottling.

Weight	
4 lb	1.8 k
1 lb	453 g
½ lb	226 g
1 oz	30 g
1 teaspoon	5 g
Liquid measure	
1 gallon	4.5 l
1 pint	568 ml
½ pint	284 ml
1 fluid oz	28 ml
1 teaspoon	5 ml

SPARKLING WINES

As you become more experienced in making your own wines new vistas will open up and eventually you will want to explore the possibility of making sparkling wines.

Certain ingredients are more suitable for sparkling wines than others: the flavour of the fruits should not be too dominant and the acidity must be fairly high. The most suitable fruits (other than grapes, of course) are gooseberries, white currants and apples. An attractive pink 'champagne' can be made with redcurrants or sloes.

The wine is made in the normal way be extracting the fruit juices and fermenting out completely. When the fermentation has ceased the clearing wine is syphoned from the lees into a sterile jar, but only a small quantity of sulphite is added—either 1 Campden tablet or 1 teaspoon of strong sulphite solution. Great care is needed in racking to prevent oxidation. When the wine is clear (after about six months) it should be racked from any sediment and prepared for the secondary fermentation. The procedure is described fully in the first recipe which follows.

PL 169208   BIN A1781   SHOP SD

SOUTHEND-ON-SEA A/N/WS AURU PB   £8.95   ISBN 1854102001

ART OF MAKING WINE

02/04/92   SAMPSON,B   PUBLISHED 01/03/92

QTY REQUIRED [   ]   1

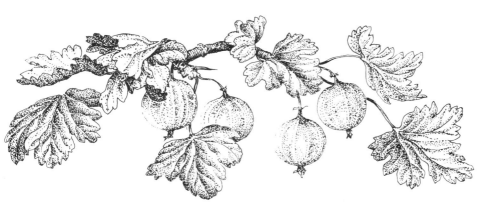

Gooseberry sparkling wine

Sulphite for sterilising   *Dissolve 8 Campden, tablets or ½ oz sodium to potassium metabisulphite in 2 pints of water and store in a screw-topped bottle.*
Strong sulphite solution   *Add 1 oz sodium or potassium metabisulphite to ½ pint water. Store in a small screw-topped bottle.*
Yeast starter bottle   *Sterilise a small bottle either by boiling for 20 minutes or filling with sterilising sulphite and leaving for 20 minutes. Pour back into the storage bottle and rinse twice to remove any sulphite solution. Half fill the bottle with cool boiled water, add the juice from half a lemon, 2 teaspoons granulated sugar and the wine yeast. Shake the bottle, plug with cotton wool and leave in a warm place of 65–70°F (18–21°C) for 48 hours.*

2½ lb gooseberries
1 lb white sultanas
1½ lb sugar
Water to 1 gallon

2 teaspoons pectin enzyme
1 teaspoon yeast nutrient
1 Vit B_1 tablet
Champagne type yeast
Campden tablets or strong sulphite
  solution

Activate the yeast starter bottle   Start records
Sterilise all equipment as required *Prepare the covered plastic bucket and utensils by washing thoroughly with warm water. Place the utensils to be used in the bucket: pour in the sterilising solution. Replace lid tightly and swirl the solution around, making sure that it reaches all parts of the bucket. Leave for 20 minutes (longer if possible) before returning the solution to the storage bottle. It will remain effective for quite a long while providing it retains its pungent odour. Carefully wash the bucket and utensils with tap water to remove all traces of sulphite before use.*

Dissolve 1 crushed Campden tablet or 1 teaspoon strong sulphite solution in 5 pints cold water. Wash the gooseberries and sultanas and liquidise lightly, using some of the 5 pints of water. Place in the fermentation bucket with the pectin enzyme, yeast nutrient and Vit B_1 tablet. Stir, cover and leave for 24 hours. Make sure the yeast starter bottle is fully active before pouring it

Weight	
4 lb	1.8 k
1 lb	453 g
½ lb	226 g
1 oz	30 g
1 teaspoon	5 g

Liquid measure	
1 gallon	4.5 l
1 pint	568 ml
½ pint	284 ml
1 fluid oz	28 ml
1 teaspoon	5 ml

carefully into one side of the bucket. (Retain a little in the starter bottle, half filling it again with a little cold water in case the bulk fails to activate.) If the active yeast starter is kept to a small area in the bucket an active colony should quickly become established, when it can be stirred into the bulk.

When the fermentation is fully active the fruit particles will be pushed to the surface by the force of the carbon dioxide being released. A sterilised plate similar in diameter to the surface of the fermenting must should be turned upside down on top to exclude the oxygen and keep the fruit particles submerged.

Break up the cap two or three times daily, replacing the lid again as quickly as possible. After 3 days strain off the liquid and pour into the fermentation jar, adding the dissolved sugar.

Fit an airlock and top up the jar with a little water after a few days. Keep in a warm place until fermentation ceases. Rack carefully and add 1 Campden tablet or 1 teaspoon strong sulphite solution.

Rack once more during the 6 months' storage period before starting the second fermentation. For this you will need a champagne yeast, activated in 5 fl oz (142 ml) of the wine and the same amount of water, with 1 fl oz (28 ml) lemon juice, 2 teaspoons sugar, a pinch of yeast nutrient and 1 Vit B$_1$ tablet.

It is of paramount importance to use heavy champagne-type bottles for all sparkling wines as considerable pressure will be built up inside them. In order to obtain the correct amount of carbon dioxide in each bottle great care must be taken over the quantity of sugar used. Too little will give only a half-hearted pop when the bottle is opened and the wine will be flat; if too much is used the cork will fly half way across the room and most of the wine will explode over the floor. The quantity of sugar used should be 3–4 oz (85–113 g) per gallon. First make sure the still wine has fermented to a specific gravity of 988 or 990. If this is the reading 4 oz of sugar may now be added; if the S.G. is 994 add only 2½ oz (70 g) (see p. 124 for scale). The S.G. reading must not exceed 1.000, preferably 998. Sweeten the bulk wine with the necessary sugar; this is best done by taking out a little wine, dissolving the sugar in it and returning it to the bulk. When the champagne

heavy bottle for sparkling

sparkling wine hydrometer readings

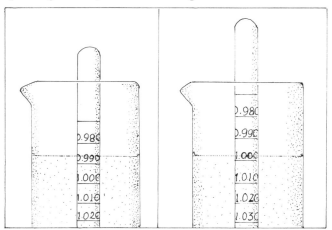

check S.G. reading
(preferably 988–990)

after addition of sugar,
S.G. 998

yeast starter is active add it to the bulk and fix an airlock. Leave in a warm place of 65°F (18°C) and as soon as there is a slight release of carbon dioxide bubbles from the airlock transfer the wine into sterile bottles, filling to within 2½ inches (6 cm) of the top of the bottle. Seal with hollow plastic sparkling wine stoppers and fix the wire cages. The bottles should be placed upside down in a crate and the crate placed in a position half way between horizontal and vertical. It is better for the temperature during the first few days to be about 55°F (13°C) increasing to 65°F (18°C).

wire cage

plastic stopper

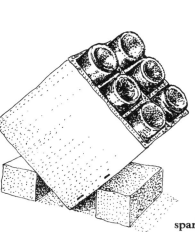

sparkling wine bottles in crate

As the secondary fermentation progresses a slight sediment will start forming on the side of the bottle, so each day the bottles should be given a short sharp twist which will gradually move the sediment down into the domed stopper. After a month most of the sediment should have settled and the wine can be moved to a cooler place, still maintaining the same position. If there is no sediment visible on the side of the bottle it will need turning only twice a week. The wine should be left on this small quantity of sediment for at least six months to acquire the distinctive flavour that is characteristic of good champagne.

An alternative method
Some winemakers experience difficulty in obtaining the secondary fermentation and it is worth trying an unorthodox method which often proves successful. In this method the ingredients for the must are prepared by extracting the juices by steeping in cold water or using a juice extractor. In order to reduce the quantity of sediment 1 gramme of Bentonite per gallon is added to the must; it is then left for 24 hours to settle before the clear liquid is racked off and the champagne yeast starter added. The wine is fermented in a warm place and when the S.G. drops to 998 is racked into a clean jar and topped up with a little cold water. It should then be removed to a cooler place (about 50°F, 10°C) for 24 hours to slow down the fermentation. The wine will clear slightly as the haze subsides to the bottom

of the jar. It must be racked again and the S.G. adjusted to 998, when it should be poured into prepared sterile champagne bottles to within 2 inches (5 cm) of the top. The procedure for storing and turning is as described above, though with this method a much larger deposit of sediment will form in the hollow domed stopper and the period needed for it to settle out will be longer, so the bottles will probably need turning for an extra month. After six to twelve months the wine will be ready for 'degorgement'.

Degorgement
It is necessary to remove the sediment inside the hollow stopper without losing the wine—an operation which is not as difficult as it may sound. If there is a deep freeze available it is easier still. Take the bottle, still upside down, and wrap the main body in a thick layer of newspaper, leaving the neck exposed and taking care not to disturb the sediment. If you have no deep freeze, invert the bottle in a large bucket of crushed ice, submerging the neck and about a third of the bottle. When the neck has partially frozen place the bottle on its side and give the hollowed stopper a quick twist to remove it, quickly placing your thumb over the end of the bottle and uprighting it. Some wine will inevitably be lost in the process and you will have to use one of the bottles for topping up the others. Top up as necessary, and insert a new sterile 'champagne' cork. Wire down and store in a cool place.

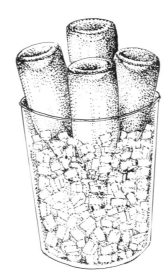

bucket with ice for degorging sediment from sparkling wine

Apple and pear sparkling wine

Sulphite for sterilising
Strong sulphite solution
Yeast starter bottle

3 lb mixed apples
3 lb pears
1 lb white sultanas
2 fl oz lemon juice
½ pint rose petals
1½ lb sugar
Water to 1 gallon

2 teaspoons pectin enzyme
1 teaspoon yeast nutrient
1 Vit B_1 tablet
Champagne type yeast
Campden tablets or strong sulphite
solution

Activate the yeast starter bottle   Start records
Sterilise all equipment as required

Dissolve 1 crushed Campden tablet or 1 teaspoon strong sulphite solution in 4 pints cold water, add the lemon juice and the washed crushed or frozen apples and pears (see p. 63). Wash the sultanas thoroughly, mince or lightly liquidise them and add with the pectin enzyme, yeast nutrient and Vit B_1 tablet. Stir well, cover and leave for 24 hours. Add the active yeast starter and when the must is fully activated pick the rose petals, crush and add to the must. Ferment on the pulp for 2 or 3 days, keeping the fruit pulp submerged. Strain, pressing the pulp, and pour into a demijohn with the dissolved sugar. Proceed as *in **Gooseberry Sparkling Wine**.

Apricot sparkling wine

Sulphite for sterilising
Strong sulphite solution
Yeast starter bottle

2 lb fresh apricots
1½ lb white sultanas
1¼ lb sugar
Water to 1 gallon

1 teaspoon pectin enzyme
1 teaspoon yeast nutrient
1 Vit B_1 tablet
Champagne type yeast
Campden tablets or strong sulphite
solution

Activate the yeast starter bottle   Start records
Sterilise all equipment as required

Wash and remove the stones from the apricots, chop them finely and place in the fermentation bucket with 1 crushed Campden tablet or 1 teaspoon strong sulphite solution and 5 pints cold water. Wash the sultanas thoroughly, mince or lightly liquidise them and add together with the pectin enzyme, yeast nutrient and Vit B_1 tablet. Stir well, cover and leave for 24 hours before adding the active yeast starter. Ferment on the pulp for 3 days, keeping the fruit well submerged. Strain, pressing the pulp lightly. Pour into a demijohn, adding the dissolved sugar. Proceed as *in **Gooseberry Sparkling Wine**.

Weight	
4 lb	1.8 k
1 lb	453 g
½ lb	226 g
1 oz	30 g
1 teaspoon	5 g

Liquid measure	
1 gallon	4.5 l
1 pint	568 ml
½ pint	284 ml
1 fluid oz	28 ml
1 teaspoon	5 ml

Grape sparkling wine

Sulphite for sterilising
Strong sulphite solution
Yeast starter bottle

10 lb white grapes (imported)
2 pints apple juice
2 fl oz lemon juice
¾ lb sugar

2 teaspoons pectin enzyme
Champagne type yeast
Campden tablets or strong sulphite
   solution

Activate the yeast starter bottle   **Start records**
Sterilise all equipment as required

Crush the grapes or lightly liquidise them in the apple juice without breaking
the seeds, add the lemon juice and 1 crushed Campden tablet or 1 teaspoon
strong sulphite solution and the pectin enzyme. Cover the fruit and leave for 24
hours. Add the active yeast starter and ferment on the pulp for 2 days, keeping
the fruit submerged at all times. Strain and press the pulp, pour into a
demijohn with the dissolved sugar. Proceed as *in **Gooseberry Sparkling
Wine**.

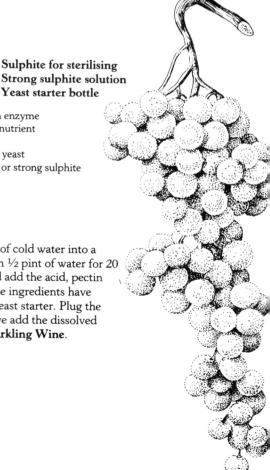

Pineapple and grape concentrate sparkling wine

Sulphite for sterilising
Strong sulphite solution
Yeast starter bottle

1 tin white grape concentrate (1 k)
1 tin pineapple juice (1 k)
3 ripe bananas
¼ oz tartaric acid
½ lb sugar
Water to 1 gallon

1 teaspoon pectin enzyme
1 teaspoon yeast nutrient
1 Vit B_1 tablet
Champagne type yeast
Campden tablets or strong sulphite
   solution

Activate the yeast starter bottle   **Start records**
Sterilise all equipment as required

Pour the grape concentrate, pineapple juice and 3 pints of cold water into a
container. Peel the bananas, slice them thinly and boil in ½ pint of water for 20
minutes. Strain the liquid into the other ingredients and add the acid, pectin
enzyme, yeast nutrient and Vit B_1 tablet. Stir until all the ingredients have
dissolved and pour into a demijohn, adding the active yeast starter. Plug the
top with cotton wool and when the fermentation is active add the dissolved
sugar and fit an airlock. Proceed as *in **Gooseberry Sparkling Wine**.

Sweet sparkling wine

Sulphite for sterilising
Strong sulphite solution
Yeast starter bottle

2 lb gooseberries and white currants (or
    gooseberries and fresh apricots)
2 lb dessert apples
1½ lb white sultanas
½ pint elderflower petals
1¼ lb sugar
Water to 1 gallon

2 teaspoons pectin enzyme
1 teaspoon yeast nutrient
1 Vit B_1 tablet
Champagne type yeast
Campden tablets or strong sulphite
    solution

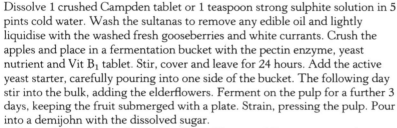

Activate the yeast starter bottle   **Start records**
Sterilise all equipment as required

Dissolve 1 crushed Campden tablet or 1 teaspoon strong sulphite solution in 5
pints cold water. Wash the sultanas to remove any edible oil and lightly
liquidise with the washed fresh gooseberries and white currants. Crush the
apples and place in a fermentation bucket with the pectin enzyme, yeast
nutrient and Vit B_1 tablet. Stir, cover and leave for 24 hours. Add the active
yeast starter, carefully pouring into one side of the bucket. The following day
stir into the bulk, adding the elderflowers. Ferment on the pulp for a further 3
days, keeping the fruit submerged with a plate. Strain, pressing the pulp. Pour
into a demijohn with the dissolved sugar.

    Proceed as *in **Gooseberry Sparkling Wine** until Degorgement, when a
sugar syrup is added to top up the bottles instead of wine. This is made by
dissolving 1 lb sugar to ½ pint water, heating slightly and stirring until
dissolved. When the sediment is removed top up the bottle with 2 fl oz of the
sugar syrup, quickly replacing a clean champagne type cork and wiring it down.

    In sweetening sparkling wines it is important that no traces of sediment
which may contain live yeast cells remain to trigger off a secondary
fermentation. After the wine is sweetened a careful check should be made
periodically to make sure there is no sediment building up in the bottle: the
wine should remain crystal clear. If in any doubt it is better to use the wine
about a month after sweetening.

Pink sparkling wine

Sulphite for sterilising
Strong sulphite solution
Yeast starter bottle

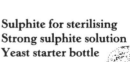

1½ lb sloes or 2 lb redcurrants
1 pint rosé grape concentrate
¾ lb sugar
Water to 1 gallon

1 teaspoon pectin enzyme
1 teaspoon yeast nutrient
1 Vit B_1 tablet
Champagne type yeast
Campden tablets or strong sulphite
    solution

Activate the yeast starter bottle   **Start records**
Sterilise all equipment as required

Crush the sloes without breaking the stones or freeze for 24 hours and place in
a fermentation bucket with 4 pints cold water and ½ crushed Campden tablet
or ½ teaspoon strong sulphite solution, the pectin enzyme, yeast nutrient and
Vit B_1 tablet. Cover and leave for 24 hours before adding the active yeast
starter. Ferment on the pulp for 2 days, keeping the fruit pulp submerged.
Strain and pour into a demijohn, adding the grape concentrate and dissolved
sugar. Proceed as *in **Gooseberry Sparkling Wine**.

    This wine is sometimes a little harsh and may be improved by the addition
of a sugar syrup as described for **Sweet Sparkling Wine**.

Weight	
4 lb	1.8 k
1 lb	453 g
½ lb	226 g
1 oz	30 g
1 teaspoon	5 g
Liquid measure	
1 gallon	4.5 l
1 pint	568 ml
½ pint	284 ml
1 fluid oz	28 ml
1 teaspoon	5 ml

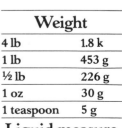

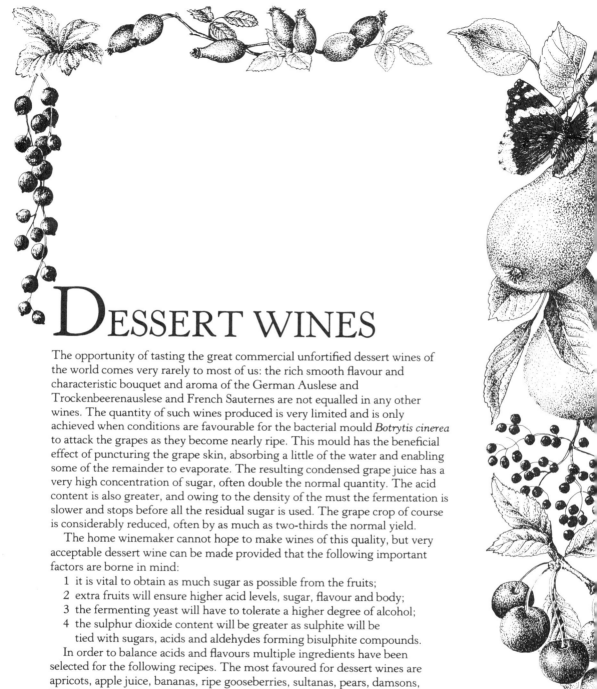

DESSERT WINES

The opportunity of tasting the great commercial unfortified dessert wines of the world comes very rarely to most of us: the rich smooth flavour and characteristic bouquet and aroma of the German Auslese and Trockenbeerenauslese and French Sauternes are not equalled in any other wines. The quantity of such wines produced is very limited and is only achieved when conditions are favourable for the bacterial mould *Botrytis cinerea* to attack the grapes as they become nearly ripe. This mould has the beneficial effect of puncturing the grape skin, absorbing a little of the water and enabling some of the remainder to evaporate. The resulting condensed grape juice has a very high concentration of sugar, often double the normal quantity. The acid content is also greater, and owing to the density of the must the fermentation is slower and stops before all the residual sugar is used. The grape crop of course is considerably reduced, often by as much as two-thirds the normal yield.

The home winemaker cannot hope to make wines of this quality, but very acceptable dessert wine can be made provided that the following important factors are borne in mind:

1 it is vital to obtain as much sugar as possible from the fruits;
2 extra fruits will ensure higher acid levels, sugar, flavour and body;
3 the fermenting yeast will have to tolerate a higher degree of alcohol;
4 the sulphur dioxide content will be greater as sulphite will be
   tied with sugars, acids and aldehydes forming bisulphite compounds.

In order to balance acids and flavours multiple ingredients have been selected for the following recipes. The most favoured for dessert wines are apricots, apple juice, bananas, ripe gooseberries, sultanas, pears, damsons, loganberries, raspberries and parsnips.

To extract as much natural sugar, acids and nutrients as possible a pulp fermentation should be carried out. In white wines the period should not exceed more than two or three days depending on the activity of the fermentation, otherwise the wine will taste rather coarse and require extra time to mature.

White dessert wines will need storing for 1–2 years before bottling and reds about 3 years.

Apricot dessert wine 1

Sulphite for sterilising   *Dissolve 8 Campden tablets or ½ oz sodium or potassium metabisulphite in 2 pints of water and store in a screw-topped bottle.*
Strong sulphite solution   *Add 1 oz sodium or potassium metabisulphite to ½ pint water. Store in a small screw-topped bottle.*
Yeast starter bottle   *Sterilise a small bottle either by boiling for 20 minutes or filling with sterilising sulphite and leaving for 20 minutes. Pour back into the storage bottle and rinse twice with cold water. Half fill the bottle with cool boiled water, add the juice from half a lemon, 2 teaspoons granulated sugar and the wine yeast. Shake the bottle, plug with cotton wool and leave in a warm place of 65–70°F (18–21°C) for 48 hours.*

3 lb fresh apricots	2 teaspoons pectin enzyme
2 lb white sultanas	1 teaspoon yeast nutrient
1 lb ripe bananas	1 Vit B$_1$ tablet
Sugar	Sauternes type yeast
Water to 1 gallon	Campden tablets or strong sulphite solution

Activate the yeast starter bottle   Start records
Sterilise all equipment as required *Prepare the covered plastic bucket and utensils by washing thoroughly with warm water. Place the utensils to be used in the bucket: pour in the sterilising solution. Replace lid tightly and swirl the solution around, making sure that it reaches all parts of the bucket. Leave for 20 minutes (longer if possible) before returning the solution to the storage bottle. It will remain effective for quite a long while providing it retains its pungent odour. Carefully wash the bucket and utensils with tap water to remove all traces of sulphite before use.*

Dissolve 1 Campden tablet or 1 teaspoon strong sulphite solution in 5 pints cold water. Chop the apricots finely, wash the sultanas thoroughly to remove the edible oils and mince; placing them all in a fermentation bucket. Thinly slice the peeled bananas and boil in 1 pint of water for 20 minutes. When cool strain off the liquid into the must, discarding the pulp. Add the pectin enzyme, yeast nutrient and Vit B$_1$ tablet. Stir, cover and leave for 24 hours. Add the active yeast starter, and when the fermentation starts and a fruit cap forms cover the surface with an upturned plate to keep the pulp submerged and exclude the oxygen. Break up the cap with the plate two or three times daily.

*After three days strain the liquid through a nylon straining bag, pressing the pulp lightly. When the liquid is strained from the pulp take a hydrometer reading and increase the specific gravity to 1.050 with sugar syrup (see p. 27). Pour the must into a demijohn, filling the jar to seven-eighths full; any surplus should be poured into a small bottle and tightly plugged with cotton wool or if the neck is large enough an airlock can be fitted. This surplus can be used for topping up the demijohn after racking at a later stage. Fit an airlock and stand the demijohn in a warm place (65–70°F, 18–21°C). Check the S.G. reading after 1 week and when it drops to 1.005 increase to 1.015 with sugar syrup. Repeat, increasing the S.G. to 1.015 until fermentation ceases. The wine can be left at an S.G. of 1.015 or increased to S.G. 1.020 according to your preference.

Syphon off the wine from the lees, adding 3 crushed Campden tablets or 3 teaspoons strong sulphite solution. If there is any surplus wine this can be used for topping up the demijohn, otherwise use a little table wine. The wine will need racking again after 2 weeks, with the addition of 2 crushed Campden tablets or 2 teaspoons of strong sulphite solution. Rack again when necessary; if care is taken there is no need to add any more sulphite.
    Mature in bulk for 2–3 years before bottling.

Weight	
4 lb	1.8 k
1 lb	453 g
½ lb	226 g
1 oz	30 g
1 teaspoon	5 g

Liquid measure	
1 gallon	4.5 l
1 pint	568 ml
½ pint	284 ml
1 fluid oz	28 ml
1 teaspoon	5 ml

Apricot dessert wine 2

Sulphite for sterilising
Strong sulphite solution
Yeast starter bottle

1 lb dried apricots
1½ lb white sultanas
1 lb ripe bananas
3 lb mixed dessert apples
4 fl oz lemon juice or ½ oz citric acid
Sugar
Water to 1 gallon

2 teaspoons pectin enzyme
1 teaspoon yeast nutrient
1 Vit B_1 tablet
Sauternes type yeast
Campden tablets or strong sulphite
    solution

Activate the yeast starter bottle   **Start records**
Sterilise all equipment as required

Dissolve 1 Campden tablet or 1 teaspoon strong sulphite solution in 5 pints cold water and pour into a fermentation bucket. Chop the washed apricots finely, wash and mince the sultanas, chop or crush the apples and place in the water with the lemon juice. Thinly slice the peeled bananas and boil in 1 pint of water for 20 minutes. Strain off the liquid into the must, adding the pectin enzyme, yeast nutrient and Vit B_1 tablet. Stir, cover and leave for 24 hours. Add the active yeast starter and when the fermentation starts and a fruit cap forms cover the surface with an upturned plate. Break up the cap two or three times daily. Proceed as *in **Dessert Apricot 1**.
    Mature in bulk for 2 years before bottling.

Apricot dessert wine 3

Sulphite for sterilising
Strong sulphite solution
Yeast starter bottle

2 tins apricots (approx. 3 lb with juice)
2 lb pears
2 lb dessert apples
1 lb sultanas
2 fl oz lemon juice
Sugar
Water to 1 gallon

2 teaspoons pectin enzyme
1 teaspoon yeast nutrient
1 Vit B_1 tablet
Sauternes type yeast
Campden tablets or strong sulphite
    solution

Activate the yeast starter bottle   **Start records**
Sterilise all equipment as required

Dissolve 1 Campden tablet or 1 teaspoon strong sulphite solution in 5 pints cold water and pour into a plastic bucket with the lemon juice. Wash and mince the sultanas, chop or crush the apples and pears and quickly place them in the bucket. Chop the apricots and add with their juice, the pectin enzyme, yeast nutrient and Vit B_1 tablet to the other ingredients. Cover and leave for 24 hours before adding the active yeast starter. Ferment on the pulp for 3 days, keeping the fruit cap submerged. Proceed as *in **Dessert Apricot 1**.

Apple dessert wine

Sulphite for sterilising
Strong sulphite solution
Yeast starter bottle

5 pints apple juice
1½ lb white sultanas
1 lb bananas
½ pint cream or yellow rose petals
2 fl oz lemon juice
Sugar
Water to 1 gallon

2 teaspoons pectin enzyme
1 teaspoon yeast nutrient
1 Vit B$_1$ tablet
Sauternes type yeast
Campden tablets or strong sulphite
  solution

Activate the yeast starter bottle   **Start records**
Sterilise all equipment as required

Wash and mince the sultanas, dissolve 1 Campden tablet or 1 teaspoon strong
sulphite solution in the apple juice, add lemon juice and put in a plastic bucket.
Thinly slice the bananas and boil in 1 pint of water for 20 minutes; strain the
liquid into the must. When cool add the pectin enzyme, yeast nutrient and Vit
B$_1$ tablet. Cover and leave for 24 hours before adding the active yeast starter.
When the fermentation is active pick the rose petals, crush and add to the
bucket. Cover the fruit cap with an upturned plate and replace the lid. Break up
the fruit cap two or three times daily. Ferment on the pulp for 3 days before
straining. Proceed as *in **Dessert Apricot 1**.

Blackberry dessert wine

Sulphite for sterilising
Strong sulphite solution
Yeast starter bottle

2 lb blackberries
2 lb sloes or 1½ lb blackcurrants
2 lb pears
1½ lb sultanas
Sugar
Water to 1 gallon

2 teaspoons pectin enzyme
1 teaspoon yeast nutrient
1 Vit B$_1$ tablet
Port or Madeira type yeast
Campden tablets or strong sulphite
  solution

Activate the yeast starter bottle   **Start records**
Sterilise all equipment as required

De-stalk and crush the blackberries, break the skins of the sloes and place in a
fermentation bucket with 5 pints cold water and 1 crushed Campden tablet or 1
teaspoon strong sulphite solution. Wash the sultanas thoroughly, mince or
lightly liquidise them in some of the 5 pints of water and return to the bucket.
Crush the pears and add with the pectin enzyme, yeast nutrient and Vit B$_1$
tablet. Stir well, cover and leave for 24 hours before adding the active yeast
starter. Ferment on the pulp for 3 days, keeping the fruit cap submerged.
Proceed as *in **Dessert Apricot 1**.
   Store at least 2 years before bottling.

Weight	
4 lb	1.8 k
1 lb	453 g
½ lb	226 g
1 oz	30 g
1 teaspoon	5 g
Liquid measure	
1 gallon	4.5 l
1 pint	568 ml
½ pint	284 ml
1 fluid oz	28 ml
1 teaspoon	5 ml

Blackcurrant dessert wine

Sulphite for sterilising
Strong sulphite solution
Yeast starter bottle

2½ lb blackcurrants
2 lb sultanas
1 lb ripe bananas
Sugar
Water to 1 gallon

2 teaspoons pectin enzyme
1 teaspoon yeast nutrient
1 Vit B_1 tablet
Port or Madeira type yeast
Campden tablets or strong sulphite
    solution

Activate the yeast starter bottle   **Start records**
Sterilise all equipment as required

Wash the sultanas thoroughly, mince or lightly liquidise them in 4 pints of cold water. Wash and crush the blackcurrants and add them to the liquid. Slice the thinly peeled bananas and boil them in 1 pint of water for 20 minutes. Add the strained liquid, the pectin enzyme, yeast nutrient, Vit B_1 tablet and 1 crushed Campden tablet or 1 teaspoon strong sulphite solution. Stir well, cover and leave for 24 hours before adding the active yeast starter. Ferment on the pulp for 5 days, keeping the fruit cap submerged with a plate. Strain and proceed as *in **Dessert Apricot 1**.

    Store 2–3 years before bottling.

Cherry dessert wine

Sulphite for sterilising
Strong sulphite solution
Yeast starter bottle

4 lb black or morello cherries
1 pint red grape concentrate
1 lb sultanas
¼ oz tartaric acid
Sugar
Water to 1 gallon

1 teaspoon pectin enzyme
1 teaspoon yeast nutrient
1 Vit B_1 tablet
Port or Madeira type yeast
Campden tablets or strong sulphite
    solution

Activate the yeast starter bottle   **Start records**
Sterilise all equipment as required

Wash the cherries and crush them, placing in a fermentation bucket with 4 pints of cold water. Wash and mince or lightly liquidise the sultanas and add with 1 crushed Campden tablet or 1 teaspoon strong sulphite solution, tartaric acid, pectin enzyme, yeast nutrient and Vit B_1 tablet. Stir, cover and leave for 24 hours. Add the active yeast starter and ferment on the pulp for 3 days, keeping the fruit cap submerged. Strain, add the grape concentrate and proceed as *in **Dessert Apricot 1**.

    Store 2 years before bottling.

Note: An 'almondy' characteristic can be achieved by cracking a few of the kernels during the initial pulp fermentation.

Damson dessert wine

Sulphite for sterilising
Strong sulphite solution
Yeast starter bottle

4 lb damsons
1 pint grape concentrate
1 lb fresh rosehips
Sugar
Water to 1 gallon

2 teaspoons pectin enzyme
1 teaspoon yeast nutrient
1 Vit B_1 tablet
Port or Madeira type yeast
Campden tablets or strong sulphite
    solution

Activate the yeast starter bottle   **Start records**
Sterilise all equipment as required

Wash and crush the damsons and rosehips and place in a fermentation bucket
with 5 pints of cold water. Add 1 crushed Campden tablet or 1 teaspoon strong
sulphite solution, the pectin enzyme, yeast nutrient and Vit B_1 tablet. Stir,
cover and leave for 24 hours. Add the active yeast starter and ferment on the
pulp for 5 days, keeping the fruit cap submerged. Strain, add the grape
concentrate and proceed as *in **Dessert Apricot 1**.

   Store at least 2 years before bottling.

Elderberry dessert wine

Sulphite for sterilising
Strong sulphite solution
Yeast starter bottle

3 lb elderberries
1 lb sloes or bullaces
1 pint red grape concentrate
1 lb sultanas
Sugar
Water to 1 gallon

1 teaspoon pectin enzyme
1 teaspoon yeast nutrient
1 Vit B_1 tablet
Port or Madeira type yeast
Campden tablets or strong sulphite
    solution

Activate the yeast starter bottle   **Start records**
Sterilise all equipment as required

Wash and mince the sultanas, crush the sloes or bullaces and place them in a
fermentation bucket with 3 pints of cold water. Add 1 crushed Campden
tablet, or 1 teaspoon strong sulphite solution, the pectin enzyme, yeast nutrient
and Vit B_1 tablet. Stir well, cover and leave for 24 hours before adding the
active yeast starter. Ferment on the pulp for 2 days, keeping the fruit cap
submerged. Crush the elderberries and place them in a stainless steel saucepan
with 3 pints of cold water; heat to 150°F (65°C), maintain this heat for 5
minutes, remove and when cool add to the must. Ferment on the pulp for a
further 2 days. Strain, pressing the pulp lightly, and add the grape concentrate.
Proceed as *in **Dessert Apricot 1**.

   Mature in bulk for 3 years before bottling.

Weight	
4 lb	1.8 k
1 lb	453 g
½ lb	226 g
1 oz	30 g
1 teaspoon	5 g

Liquid measure	
1 gallon	4.5 l
1 pint	568 ml
½ pint	284 ml
1 fluid oz	28 ml
1 teaspoon	5 ml

Gooseberry dessert wine

Sulphite for sterilising
Strong sulphite solutio
Yeast starter bottle

2 lb sweet gooseberries
1 lb green gooseberries
2 lb pears
2 lb white sultanas
Sugar
Water to 1 gallon

2 teaspoons pectin enzyme
1 teaspoon yeast nutrient
1 Vit B_1 tablet
Sauternes type yeast
Campden tablets or strong sulphite
  solution

Activate the yeast starter bottle   **Start records**
Sterilise all equipment as required

Wash and crush the gooseberries and place in a fermentation bucket with 5
pints of cold water, adding 1 crushed Campden tablet or 1 teaspoon strong
sulphite solution. Wash the sultanas thoroughly, either mince or lightly
liquidise them and add to the crushed gooseberries. Crush the pears, adding
them with the pectin enzyme, yeast nutrient and Vit B_1 tablet. Stir, cover and
leave for 24 hours. Add the active yeast starter and ferment on the pulp for 3
days, keeping the fruit submerged. Strain and proceed as *in **Dessert
Apricot 1**.

  Mature in bulk for 3 years before bottling.

Loganberry or raspberry dessert wine

Sulphite for sterilising
Strong sulphite solution
Yeast starter bottle

2 lb loganberries or 3 lb raspberries
1 lb pears
1 lb bananas
1 pint red grape concentrate
Sugar
Water to 1 gallon

1 teaspoon pectin enzyme
1 teaspoon yeast nutrient
1 Vit B_1 tablet
Port or Madeira type yeast
Campden tablets or strong sulphite
  solution

Activate the yeast starter bottle   **Start records**
Sterilise all equipment as required

Crush the loganberries and pears and place them in a fermentation bucket with
4 pints of cold water, adding 1 crushed Campden tablet or 1 teaspoon strong
sulphite solution. Peel the bananas, slice thinly and boil in 1 pint of water for
20 minutes; strain the liquid into the fruit pulp and when cool add the pectin
enzyme, yeast nutrient and Vit B_1 tablet. Stir well, cover and leave for 24 hours.
Add the active yeast starter and ferment on the pulp for 3 days, keeping the
fruit cap submerged. Strain, add the grape concentrate, stirring until it has
dissolved, and proceed as **Dessert Apricot 1**.

  Mature in bulk for 2–3 years before bottling.

Note: Raspberries can be used instead of loganberries: they are very similar in
composition, but as they contain a little less acid you should use 3 lb for a
gallon of wine.

Orange dessert wine

Sulphite for sterilising
Strong sulphite solution
Yeast starter bottle

3 pints pure orange juice
2 lb white sultanas
1 lb bananas
½ lb light coloured English honey
Sugar
Water to 1 gallon

2 teaspoons pectin enzyme
1 teaspoon yeast nutrient
1 Vit B_1 tablet
Bordeaux type yeast
Campden tablets or strong sulphite
  solution

Activate the yeast starter bottle   **Start records**
Sterilise all equipment as required

Wash the sultanas thoroughly to remove the edible oils, mince or lightly
liquidise them in a little water. Squeeze the oranges, thinly slicing the outside
peel from one; add to the sultanas. Slice the peeled bananas and boil for 20
minutes in 2 pints of water. Strain the liquid and add this also. Crush 1
Campden tablet or 1 teaspoon strong sulphite solution and add with the pectin
enzyme, yeast nutrient and Vit B_1 tablet. Stir well, cover and leave for 24 hours.
Add the active yeast starter and ferment on the pulp for 3 days, keeping the
pulp submerged. Strain and add the honey, stirring until dissolved. Proceed as
Dessert Apricot 1.
   Mature in bulk for 3 years before bottling.

Parsnip dessert wine

Sulphite for sterilising
Strong sulphite solution
Yeast starter bottle

4 lb parsnips
3 pints apple juice or 4 lb mixed apples
1½ lb white sultanas
1 lb ripe bananas
2 oz preserved angelica
½ oz tartaric acid
Sugar
Water to 1 gallon

2 teaspoons pectin enzyme
1 teaspoon yeast nutrient
1 Vit B_1 tablet
Sauternes type yeast
Campden tablets or strong sulphite
  solution

Activate the yeast starter bottle   **Start records**
Sterilise all equipment as required

Wash and scrub the parsnips, slice them thinly and place in a saucepan with 6
pints cold water (or 7 pints if using apples, not apple juice). Skin the bananas,
slice and add. Bring to the boil and boil gently for 30 minutes without the lid.
Strain from the pulp and leave to settle. After 24 hours syphon the clear liquid
from the sediment. Wash and mince the sultanas and add them with the apple
juice or washed, crushed apples to the liquid, with 1 crushed Campden tablet
or 1 teaspoon strong sulphite solution, the tartaric acid, pectin enzyme, yeast
nutrient and Vit B_1 tablet. Stir well, cover and leave for 24 hours. Add the
active yeast starter and ferment on the pulp for 3 days, keeping the fruit pulp
submerged. Strain and proceed as **Dessert Apricot 1**, with one exception.
When the S.G. has been taken and the must poured into the demijohn the
angelica is infused in the wine. It should be thinly sliced and placed in a small
open-mesh bag weighted with a marble. Tie the top of the bag with a piece of
cotton, leaving long ends for suspending the bag in the wine. Leave for 7 days,
each day removing the airlock and giving the cotton attachment a few jerks to
distribute the flavour.
   Mature in bulk for 3 years before bottling.

Weight	
4 lb	1.8 k
1 lb	453 g
½ lb	226 g
1 oz	30 g
1 teaspoon	5 g
Liquid measure	
1 gallon	4.5 l
1 pint	568 ml
½ pint	284 ml
1 fluid oz	28 ml
1 teaspoon	5 ml

Peach dessert wine

Sulphite for sterilising
Strong sulphite solution
Yeast starter bottle

3 lb peaches
2 lb ripe bananas
1 pint white grape concentrate
1 lb pears
½ oz tartaric acid
Sugar
Water to 1 gallon

2 teaspoons pectin enzyme
1 teaspoon yeast nutrient
1 Vit B_1 tablet
Sauternes or Bordeaux type yeast
Campden tablets or strong sulphite
  solution

Activate the yeast starter bottle   Start records
Sterilise all equipment as required

Peel and thinly slice the bananas and boil them in 2 pints of water for 20
minutes. Strain, discarding the pulp. Slice the peaches, crush the pears and add
them with 3 pints of cold water to the fermentation bucket. Crush 1 Campden
tablet or 1 teaspoon strong sulphite solution, and add with the tartaric acid,
pectin enzyme, yeast nutrient and Vit B_1 tablet. Stir well, cover and leave for 24
hours. Add the active yeast starter and ferment on the pulp for 3 days, keeping
the fruit cap submerged. Strain and add the grape concentrate, stirring until it
has dissolved. Proceed as for **Dessert Apricot 1**.
    Mature in bulk for 2 years before bottling.

Pear dessert wine

Sulphite for sterilising
Strong sulphite solution
Yeast starter bottle

4 lb cooking pears
2 lb crab apples
2 lb white sultanas
3 vanilla pods
Sugar
Water to 1 gallon

2 teaspoons pectin enzyme
1 teaspoon yeast nutrient
1 Vit B_1 tablet
Sauternes or Bordeaux type yeast
Campden tablets or strong sulphite
  solution

Activate the yeast starter bottle   Start records
Sterilise all equipment as required

Wash the sultanas thoroughly, mince or lightly liquidise them and place in a
fermentation bucket with 5 pints cold water and 1 crushed Campden tablet or 1
teaspoon strong sulphite solution. Add the pectin enzyme, yeast nutrient and
Vit B_1 tablet. Stir well, cover and leave for 24 hours, keeping the pulp
submerged. Add the active yeast starter and ferment on the pulp for 3 days,
taking care to keep the fruit cap submerged. Strain and proceed as *in **Dessert
Apricot 1**. The vanilla pods should be infused in the demijohn for 7–10 days.
    Mature in bulk for 2 years before bottling.

Note: If crab apples are unobtainable use 2 lb mixed apples and 4 fl oz lemon
juice or 3 teaspoons malic acid.

Sloe dessert wine

Sulphite for sterilising
Strong sulphite solution
Yeast starter bottle

3 lb sloes
2 lb ripe bananas
1 pint red grape concentrate
Sugar
Water to 1 gallon

2 teaspoons pectin enzyme
1 teaspoon yeast nutrient
1 Vit B_1 tablet
Port type yeast
Campden tablets or strong sulphite
    solution

Activate the yeast starter bottle   **Start records**
Sterilise all equipment as required

Wash the sloes and place them in a stainless steel saucepan with 4 pints of cold water. Heat to 150°F (65°C), maintaining the heat for 10 minutes. Thinly slice the peeled bananas and boil in 1½ pints water for 20 minutes, straining the liquid into the sloes. When the sloes are cool break the skins and add the pectin enzyme, yeast nutrient, Vit B_1 tablet and active yeast starter. Ferment on the pulp for 2 days, keeping the fruit cap submerged. Strain and add the grape concentrate, stirring until dissolved. Proceed as for **Dessert Apricot 1**.

    Mature in bulk for 3 years before bottling.

Strawberry dessert wine

Sulphite for sterilising
Strong sulphite solution
Yeast starter bottle

3 lb strawberries
1 lb blackcurrants
2 lb white sultanas
Sugar
Water to 1 gallon

2 teaspoons pectin enzyme
1 teaspoon yeast nutrient
1 Vit B_1 tablet
Port or Madeira type yeast
Campden tablets or strong sulphite
    solution

Activate the yeast starter bottle   **Start records**
Sterilise all equipment as required

Wash the sultanas thoroughly, mince or lightly liquidise them in 4 pints cold water. Crush the strawberries and blackcurrants and place them in a fermentation bucket with 1 crushed Campden tablet or 1 teaspoon strong sulphite solution, the pectin enzyme, yeast nutrient, Vit B_1 tablet. Stir well, cover and leave for 24 hours. Add the active yeast starter. Ferment on the pulp for 3 days, keeping the fruit cap submerged. Proceed as *in **Dessert Apricot 1**.

    Mature in bulk for 2 years before bottling.

Weight	
4 lb	1.8 k
1 lb	453 g
½ lb	226 g
1 oz	30 g
1 teaspoon	5 g

Liquid measure	
1 gallon	4.5 l
1 pint	568 ml
½ pint	284 ml
1 fluid oz	28 ml
1 teaspoon	5 ml

GRAPES

Growing, development and care

As you gain confidence in making country wines you will probably wish to try your hand at grape wines and will therefore look at the possibilities of growing your own grapes. Vines have been grown successfully in greenhouses and out of doors in southern parts of Great Britain over many centuries. Most houses with a garden will have an area suitable for growing a few vines in the open or a greenhouse large enough to take one or two.

If you plan to grow vines in the open you must give careful consideration to choosing the most suitable site. The first point to remember is that the vine is a worshipper of the sun; this obviously presents problems for the British grower, but much can be done to make certain that your vines get the best of any sun that is available. Against a wall is an ideal site, as the wall will shelter the vine and reflect vital heat. If a larger area is planned choose a site out of the prevailing wind, preferably on a slope facing south, so that the vines may benefit from the first rays of sunshine in the morning right through to the last as the sun sinks in the evening. Warmth is of paramount importance but so is shelter, as cooling winds will prevent the vines' development and production. Great care must be taken however to ensure that the site is not in a frost pocket, as this could be very damaging in late spring or early summer when the buds are bursting.

As the roots of the vine penetrate deeply into the soil and spread laterally over a large area the soil structure is of great importance if the feeder roots are to absorb sufficient water and nutrients from the soil. They will not thrive in heavy water-logged conditions but will remain stinted and may eventually die. Soils cannot be exchanged but they can be changed. If the only site available is of clay this can be improved by laying drains at least 15 inches (40 cm) below the surface to remove excessive water. A mixture of straw compost, lime, peat and sand should then be worked in to increase the humus content, and this will eventually help to aerate the soil. Soils which consist mainly of chalk or lime can be improved with a generous application of humus, bone meal and potash, but vines planted in this type of soil should be grafted on specially selected root stocks grown for this purpose.

Most garden soils consist mainly of medium loam, loamy sand or gravel. These can only be described as the perfect medium in which the vine flourishes, provided that attention is paid to liming the soil when the pH drops below 6.5 and that normal levels of phosphorus and potassium are maintained.

Varieties

Before planting, due consideration should be given to the pros and cons of different varieties of vine. Many new varieties of German, Alsace and French vines were introduced into this country after the Second World War and planted for the first time in various parts of southern England, both in gardens and commercial vineyards. As the commercial vineyards are scattered over a wide area climatic conditions vary considerably and many varieties that produce well in one area have failed completely in another.

The most important attribute for an outdoor vine is that it should produce good ripe wood, enabling the fruiting buds to be laid down and develop. In the ensuing year the vine should have a minimum of cultural faults, allowing one or two bunches of flowers per lateral branch with a good fruit set and the ability to ripen its fruit within a reasonable period. Some vines are more susceptible to diseases than others, the most common being powdery and downy mildews and botrytis, so unless a systematic spraying programme can be carried out it is advisable to choose varieties that have a high resistance to these diseases.

All varieties have a credit and a debit side depending on the season, so the decision must be left to the viticulturist to select which he considers most suitable for the site available.

The *Muller Thurgau* variety was very popular a few years ago but has lost favour during recent cold, wet summers by its inability to ripen its canes before the winter, resulting in soft green wood with diseases being carried through the winter and poor flowering the following year.

The hybrid variety *Seyval Blanc* will produce a crop when many others fail, but it does need good weather in the period prior to and at flowering time. The sugar content of the juice is rather low, however, and the wine often proves disappointing. It is a useful vine to grow for blending with other more pronounced and characteristic varieties.

Reichensteiner has the advantage that even in difficult cold years it will have a good flower set and the bunches of grapes are open, giving good resistance against botrytis. The wood ripens adequately most years and the grapes produce a very light, refreshing wine.

Madeleine Angevine 7672 has produced well in many English vineyards. It has few cultural problems and produces good ripe wood. The advantage of growing Madeleine Angevine in cooler climates is its ability to ripen early, taking approximately 80 days from fruit set to harvest compared with 90–100 days for most varieties.

Regner is a more recently introduced variety to Britain. It has vigorous growth and is a heavy cropper, but prone to botrytis. It sets its fruit better than most other varieties in Britain and produces a well-balanced wine.

Schönburger has gained favour in many commercial vineyards in the last few years. It is a fairly late ripener but produces an excellent white wine, which matures early with a pronounced Muscat flavour.

Siegerrebe will thrive on most sites, but with the grapes ripening early they are susceptible to wasp damage. If weather conditions are poor at flowering time the bunches may fail to set. Although a fairly low cropper, its grapes contain a high sugar content and they are ideally suited for sweet types of wine with a strong Muscat flavour.

Huxelrebe thrives in warm, sheltered sites but dislikes cold, windy conditions. Growth is vigorous and grapes ripen fairly early, but its main drawback is the high acidity of the juice.

Outdoor red varieties   *Dornfelder*, which is of German origin, is the best variety to grow outside. It is easy to grow, has few disease problems and will ripen well in our climate. The wine produced is deep-coloured with a good balance of acidity in most vintages, and it has the additional advantage of producing relatively high yields.

Other red varieties that can be grown outdoors are Dunkelfelder and Triomphe d'Alsace and, on favourable sites, Zweigeltrebe is recommended.

Planting

The vine will need some form of support as it matures. The type of support needed in a garden will depend on the site available. The vines can be planted and supported in rows, trellised over an existing porch, or if only a restricted area is available a Goblet type support may be used. Many English vineyards favour planting the vines in rows and training them in what is called the Double Guyot system (see p. 114). In this system the vines are planted 4 foot (1.2 m) apart with 6 foot (1.8 m) between rows, but if small cultivators are used or cultivation is done by hand the rows can be closer together, i.e. 5 foot (1.5 m).

Unless the vines are pot grown they should be planted in the autumn or late spring depending on the severity of the winter. Grafted vines from the Continent are imported in the spring, when planting should be carried out as quickly as possible. Dig a hole about 12 inches (30 cm) in diameter and about 15 inches (38 cm) deep. Break up the bottom of the hole with a fork and replace about 3 inches (7 cm) of top soil. Insert a long bamboo cane which will act as a marker and eventual support for the vine in its first two years. If the roots are longer than 6 inches (15 cm) cut them back to this length. Place the vine in the centre of the hole, fanning the roots out in all directions. If the vine has been grafted the waxed bulge near the top should be level with the surrounding surface. Fill in the hole and firm the soil, carefully covering the graft scar with a little soil to prevent drying out or other damage during the first year.

Pruning

Vines take about three to four years to become established before they are able to bear a useful crop of grapes. The root systems may be expected to develop at the same rate as the top growth, so if the vine has failed to generate sufficient canes and leaves the roots also will be underdeveloped. The soil nutrient and general growing conditions must be checked, and in the dormant period the canes should be pruned back to encourage the root system. A lot of patience is required in these first few years to train and develop a healthy vine that will give a potential crop for twenty to twenty-five years.

There are several different methods of pruning, depending on the available site and number of vines grown.

Double Guyot system In the first year the buds will start to burst in April or early May. Select two of the strongest shoots and rub off the remainder. When they reach about 6 inches (15 cm) again select the strongest shoot, removing the other. As the cane grows pinch out all the side shoots after the first leaf in the bottom 3 foot (1 m) of cane and support it by tying at intervals loosely to the bamboo; this will prevent damage caused by wind. When the cane reaches 5 feet (1.5 m) pinch off the top.

The following January if the cane has not made very much growth it should be pruned back to three or four buds, repeating the process of the first year. If, however, a good strong cane has been produced which is hard and thicker than a pencil, it should be cut at 15 inches (38 cm) to form the stock or trunk of the vine. This is the permanent stem which will grow in diameter each year by adding a new layer of wood. The stock or trunk plays an important part as the connecting link between the roots and fruiting canes, not only in supporting

The Double Guyot system

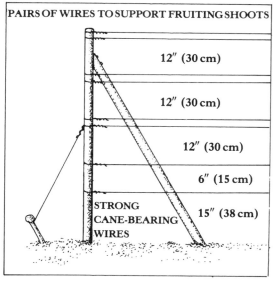

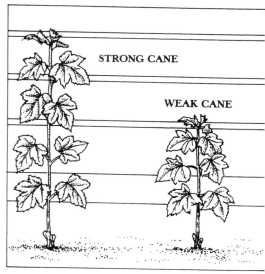

first year   following summer

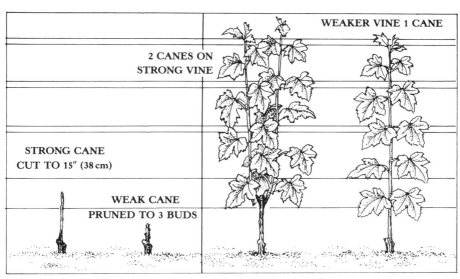

2 CANES ON
STRONG VINE

WEAKER VINE 1 CANE

STRONG CANE
CUT TO 15" (38 cm)

WEAK CANE
PRUNED TO 3 BUDS

second year pruning — following summer

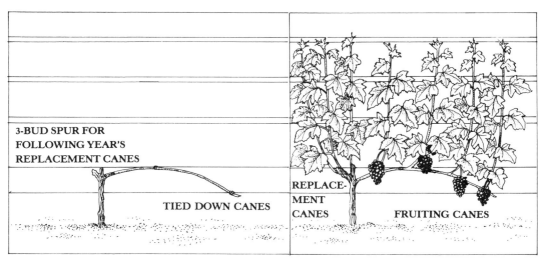

3-BUD SPUR FOR
FOLLOWING YEAR'S
REPLACEMENT CANES

TIED DOWN CANES

REPLACE-
MENT
CANES

FRUITING CANES

third year pruning — following summer

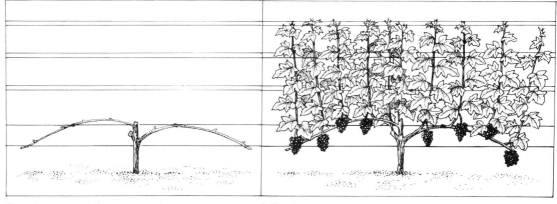

fourth year and future pruning — following summer

Training against a wall

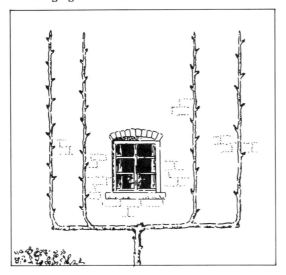 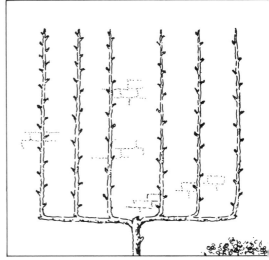

vertical cordons

them at the desired height from the ground but acting as a channel that supplies water and nutrients from the roots to the developing vine.

In the second year when the buds burst rub out all but two of the strongest near the top of the stock. As they grow tuck them into the supporting wires. Remove any side shoots at the base of the canes, and when they reach 5 feet (1.5 m) pinch off the tops.

The following January select the strongest cane, cut to 2 feet (60 cm) from the head of the stock and tie firmly to the bottom wire. Cut the remaining cane to three buds; this will provide good strong shoots and cane near the stock for replacement canes the following year. As the buds burst the next spring the shoots will grow quickly and must be tucked in between the supporting wires. If the vine produces more than eight or ten flower sets per vine in this third year, remove a few bunches otherwise all the energy will be directed into producing grapes at this early stage rather than developing a good rooting system which is essential for the long-term production of the vine.

Pruning in the fourth year forms the basis for all future pruning. Select two of the strongest canes near the stock and cut them back to 2–2½ feet (60–76 cm). Choose a third cane and cut it back to a three-bud spur, thus ensuring the following years' replacement canes. Remove all remaining wood and tie down the two new fruiting canes.

Goblet   If you have only a restricted area available or want to plant vines in odd corners of the garden you should practise 'Head' or 'Goblet' pruning. The advantages of this method are simplicity of form and low costs. The vine is grown as in the first year of the Double Guyot system, but two three-bud spurs are left at the first pruning and four spurs the following year; these should be distributed in different parts at the head of the stock to avoid later crowding of the fruit. A 5 foot (1.5 m) stake is erected close to the vine and the growing laterals are tied to this for support.

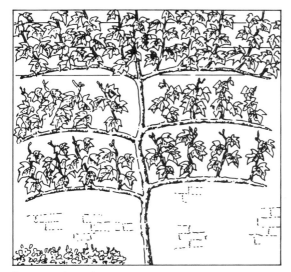

horizontal cordons

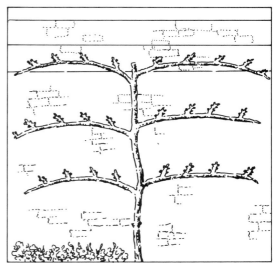

prune the spurs, leaving buds on each spur

Training vines on walls   Vines can be grown successfully on a south-facing wall by training them as a vertical or horizontal cordon. A large expanse of brickwork on the side of a house or garden wall can be covered by a number of horizontal cordons at different levels.

The vines should be spaced up to 12 feet (3.6 m) apart, and as the canes grow they can be attached to the wall forming a permanent framework. The fruit is borne on spurs, growing from the main canes, and these should be cut back annually to three or four buds. Where wall space is limited a vertical cordon may be suitable, perhaps using the space each side of a window.

Head or goblet pruning

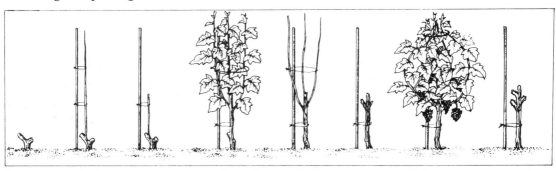

| first year | end of first year | prune to form permanent stock | second year's summer growth | end of second year | prune to 3 spurs | third year's summer growth | prune to 4 spurs, leaving 2–3 buds on each spur |

Diseases

Most of the diseases that affect the vine thrive in warm humid conditions. With a heavy rainfall in Britain we cannot escape these problems, so a spraying routine must be evolved to combat the most predominant diseases, i.e. mildews and botrytis.

Powdery mildew (Oidium)   This is identified by fine, grey, translucent cobweb-like patches on the leaves. As the colonies develop a musty odour is transmitted. The disease can be prevented by spraying with Supercarb or Benlate. It should be applied when the shoots are about 6 inches (15 cm) high and applied every 14 days until a month before harvest.

Downy mildew (Plasmopara)   The first evidence of infection is small patches of white mildew which form on the underside of the leaf. As the disease develops the affected part of the leaf turns brown, finally becoming brittle and eventually falling off. In severely affected vines the shoots, tendrils and stems may also be attacked which causes considerable damage to the vine. In damp weather conditions a spray of Dithane or Bordeaux mixture, which contains copper sulphate, should be applied. The first application should be made just before flowering, one after flowering and another 14 days later.

Botrytis   This may affect the fruit if moist and humid conditions prevail as the fruit ripens, particularly if the grapes have split or are damaged in any way. The grey mould attacks the damaged fruit, quickly spreading to the remaining berries and covering them with a mass of grey to buff-coloured spores. If the attack takes place when the grapes are nearly ripe the affected grapes can be

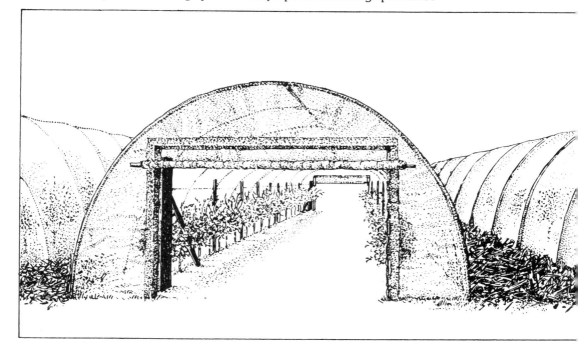

vines growing in polythene tunnels

used to make wine even though they may look very unappetising. (These are in fact the grapes which are left on the vine in Sauternes and Germany to dry out and make the lovely dessert wines.) The disease should not present too great a problem and can be controlled by using one of the proprietary sprays, e.g. Benlate or Supercarb, before flowering and two weeks after flowering. It is advisable to spray again at fortnightly intervals if the weather conditions are hot and humid.

Growing under cover

In good seasons vines will flourish and produce favourable crops in the open, but after several adverse summers resulting in poor crops and high acid levels the introduction of an alternative method became a necessity in our Devon vineyard. In 1980 we decided to experiment by covering some of our existing vines with polythene tunnels. By 1991 approximately 1,000 vines (10 per cent of the total vineyard) had been covered. The varieties which have consistently produced heavily in the polytunnels are Reichensteiner, Muller Thurgau, Bacchus, Scheurebe and Gutenborner. In our experience the vines should increase their annual yield by more than 100 per cent, and the quality of the grapes has also improved considerably, with lower acid levels. Mildews and botrytis, which were anticipated as a major problem, have been easily kept under control, with far less incidence than suffered by the outside vines. None of the varieties experienced any flowering or setting problems, and produced full bunches.

More recently late-ripening varieties have been planted in order to be covered

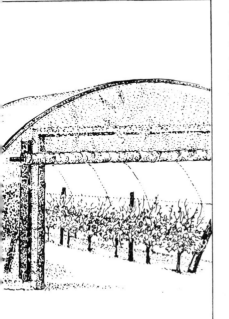

Calculating degree days

Degree days are calculated by taking the mean monthly temperature above 50°F (10°C): this is the base-line set because no growth takes place below this temperature. The growing period is calculated over the period 1 April to 31 October.

To arrive at the mean temperature take the maximum day temperature and the minimum night temperature and divide by two. When the 'no growth' temperature of 50°F (10°C) has been subtracted, the figure left represents the degree days. For example:

maximum day temperature 65°F	18°C
minimum night temperature 51°F	10.5°C
mean temp. = (65 + 51) ÷ 2 = 58°F	(18 + 10.5) ÷ 2 = 14.25°C
degree days = 58°F − 50°F = **8**	14.25 − 10 = **4.25**

This figure represents 8 degree days on the Fahrenheit scale and 4.25 degree days on the Centigrade scale.

Add together the daily degree days to give the monthly figure, and at the end of the season the monthly figures can be totalled to give the degree days for the season.

with polytunnels. It is too early at this stage to know which varieties will perform best, but the white varieties in the trial include Ehrenfelser and Kerner, both marginally too late in ripening for growing outdoors in Britain, and the classic Continental white varieties – Riesling, Chardonnay and Gewürztraminer.

From our experience of red varieties, clearly the most successful have been the classic Bordeaux red varieties, Cabernet Sauvignon and Merlot. The varieties suitable for polytunnels should also be suitable for greenhouses and conservatories.

The important advantages have been the health of the vines, abundant flowering, good setting of the fruit and ripening within a reasonable period. This we attribute to the considerable increase in degree days compared with the open vineyard. In Devon we are affected by a maritime climate, warmer than average in winter and spring but cooler in the summer on account of breezes coming off the sea. The degree days in the open vineyard over a number of years have averaged between 780 C and 850 C compared with the polytunnels at 1500 C. To get a consistent crop in Britain at least 800 C degree days are required, slightly lower than the northern parts of Germany or at Reims in France, where the average degree days are 900–1000 C.

The project has attracted a lot of interest from other growers who wish to enhance the quality of their wine. The idea of growing grapes much further north becomes a practical possibility when even in poor seasons a regular crop of ripe grapes can be achieved.

The amateur gardener can do a great deal to protect his vines against the elements at flowering time by using heavy-gauge polythene secured over the top of a wooden frame. This will ensure a good flower set and extra heat to ripen the grapes. The ends of the frame should remain open to allow a free flow of air, preventing mildews and excessive heat which could damage the vine.

Commercial vineyards

The English vineyards have received considerable attention over the past ten years. They have combated unfavourable weather conditions, pests and cultural diseases and experimented with varieties of vines introduced from the Continent. This has involved considerable work and expense with many failures, but certain patterns are now evolving and with viticulturists pooling their experiences and information varieties will eventually be found to suit our inhospitable climate. What is surprising is that even in poor years when the grapes are not harvested until November delightful wines can still be produced.

The vintage

Whether only one vine is grown or many hundreds, the romanticism of the harvest appeals to most people. It is the viticulturist alone, however, who bears the responsibility of deciding when the grapes are ready to pick. Is the specific gravity high enough or has the acid dropped to an acceptable level? Can bird and wasp damage be risked for another few days? Will the deep storm depression that is forecast completely devastate the vintage crop? All these factors must be considered in deciding when the harvest will take place. In commercial vineyards an instrument called a refractometer is used to test the sugar content of the grapes; as the grapes vary even on the same bunch it is essential to test several grapes from different bunches. For small-scale growers an accurate idea of the sugar content may be gained by picking a few bunches, squeezing out the juice and taking the specific gravity reading with a hydrometer.

Two or three days before picking, the yeast starter bottle should be prepared: use a cultured Mosel or Hock type yeast for white wines and a Bordeaux or Burgundy for reds. If a large quantity of grapes is to be harvested the amount of yeast should be increased by picking some grapes and hand processing them to obtain a few gallons of juice to activate. This can be done by crushing the berries gently, placing them in a double nylon net bag and wringing the juice out by hand.

When the grapes are picked, remove them from the stalks and crush lightly, adding 1 Campden tablet or 1 teaspoon (5 ml) strong sulphite solution per gallon of crushed grapes; this is important as the juice and grapes oxidise very quickly. If a press is available the grapes can be pressed immediately but if they are to be hand processed add 1 heaped teaspoon of pectin-destroying enzyme and leave in a covered plastic bucket or container for 24 hours before pressing in a nylon bag. Most English grape juice will require the addition of sugar, so a specific gravity reading must be taken to ascertain the quantity of sugar needed to bring the S.G. up to 1.085.

If you are in doubt about the acidity of the juice, or if you are making more than a few gallons, it is worth buying an acid testing kit. Most of these are expressed as percentage of sulphuric acid, and if a reading of over 0.55 per cent is recorded the acidity of the juice will need correction. Some acid testing kits are expressed as grammes per litre, however, and this quantity would then read 5.5 grammes per litre.

The predominant acids in grape must are tartaric and malic, with a high proportion of malic acid in poor years. Precipitated chalk is often used to neutralise some of the acid, but as tartaric acid will be the first to be neutralised care should be taken not to overdo the quantity used. Reducing acid in this way will be necessary in a very poor year, but it can only be described as a retrograde step and should not be practised normally. If the grapes consistently have such high acid levels steps should be taken either to replace them with an earlier variety or to cover them in order to increase the heat levels.

Most grapes grown in Britain are white and the juice is therefore fermented in the normal way by extracting the juice and fermenting in anaerobic conditions. If red grapes are grown for rosé or red wine, fermentation will take place on the pulp; usually three days is long enough for rosé wines, but ten to fourteen days will be necessary for the deep reds. With pulp fermentations always keep the container tightly sealed and the fruit pulp submerged, thus ensuring a better extraction rate from the fruit and less risk of bacterial infection.

Imported grapes
Growing their own grapes and making their own wine is the ultimate achievement for most winemakers, but if you live in an area unsuitable for growing vines or in an urban environment this may be impossible. Alternatives can be found: table grapes are imported in large quantities, and with today's

speed of transport their condition on arrival is generally excellent. The wines made from table grapes will not achieve the distinctive characteristic flavour of the wine grape varieties, however, as table grapes are grown to produce large fleshy berries which are picked as soon as they reach the minimum degree of maturity. Their development ceases as soon as they are picked and they never reach their full potential in flavour, colour or texture, so other ingredients will be needed to compensate for this lack.

Most grapes imported into Britain are from Spain or Algeria and therefore have received the optimum amount of sunshine; acidity will consequently be low and will need increasing to obtain an interesting wine. As they are picked before they reach their highest sugar potential this will also need adjustment. It is often better to wait for a mid-season importation when the grapes will have reached a higher level of maturity. More flavour and character will be imparted to this wine if the grapes are fermented on the pulp for a few days before pressing.

Many interesting wines can be made by adding a few garden or hedgerow fruits to the grapes. Three-quarters of a pound (340 g) of gooseberries per gallon in white varieties will usually give the required amount of acidity and will produce a far superior wine; half a pound (225 g) of sloes, blackcurrants or bullaces improves the insipid character of some red varieties. The winemaker thus has great opportunities to improve and enhance each year's vintage, a challenge that will provide interest and enjoyment from the moment the first fruits are gathered to the drinking of the finished wine.

Recipes

Before harvesting the grapes take a few bunches at random, crush and squeeze out the juice and take an S.G. reading. If you have a large quantity of grapes you should buy an acid testing kit, taking care to follow the accompanying instructions. The acid levels are sometimes expressed as tartaric acid, in which case 8.5 g per litre is acceptable; if they are expressed as sulphuric acid the reading should be 5–5.5 g per litre.

When the levels are satisfactory you may begin to harvest, but if the acidity is still too high and the S.G. too low it is advisable to wait a little longer for the quality to improve.

Grape, white

Sulphite for sterilising
Strong sulphite solution
Yeast starter bottle

15 lb white grapes
Sugar to adjust

2 teaspoons pectin enzyme
Hock type yeast
Campden tablets or strong sulphite solution

Activate the yeast starter bottle   Start records
Sterilise all equipment as required

Pick the grapes, remove them from the stalks and place in a plastic bucket. If the grapes are fully ripe they can be crushed easily by hand or with a sterilised wooden block. Add the pectin enzyme and 1 crushed Campden tablet or 1 teaspoon strong sulphite solution. Stir well, cover with an upturned plate, then cover the bucket and leave for 24 hours. Press the grapes or strain through a strong nylon straining bag, squeezing the bag to extract all the juice. Take an S.G. reading of the juice and adjust with sugar syrup to 1.080. Pour into a demijohn and add the active yeast starter. Plug the jar with cotton wool and when the fermentation is active replace with an airlock.

Leave in a warm place and when the fermentation ceases (10–14 days) rack the clearing wine from the lees in a clean jar and remove to a cool place. After 2 days rack again, adding 2 Campden tablets or 2 teaspoons strong sulphite solution; fit a cork bung. Rack again when a heavy deposit forms, adding another Campden tablet or 1 teaspoon strong sulphite solution.

Mature in bulk for 12 months before bottling.

Grape, red

Sulphite for sterilising
Strong sulphite solution
Yeast starter bottle

15 lb red grapes
Sugar to adjust

2 teaspoons pectin enzyme
Burgundy or Bordeaux type yeast
Campden tablets or strong sulphite solution

Activate the yeast starter bottle   Start records
Sterilise all equipment as required

Pick the grapes, remove them from the stalks and place in a plastic bucket. Crush the grapes by hand or with a sterilised wooden block. Add the pectin enzyme and 1 crushed Campden tablet or 1 teaspoon strong sulphite solution. Stir, cover with an upturned plate, then cover the bucket and leave for 24 hours. Strain a little juice to take the S.G. reading and adjust with sugar syrup to 1.090. Add the active yeast starter and ferment on the pulp for 7 days, keeping the fruit submerged with the plate and the bucket tightly covered. Break up the fruit cap two or three times daily. Strain and pour into a demijohn and fit an airlock.

When fermentation ceases rack the clearing wine from the lees into a clean jar and remove to a cool place. After 2 days rack again, adding 2 Campden tablets or 2 teaspoons strong sulphite solution; fit a cork bung. Rack again when a heavy deposit forms, adding another Campden tablet or 1 teaspoon strong sulphite solution.

Mature in bulk for 18 months before bottling.

Weight	
4 lb	1.8 k
1 lb	453 g
½ lb	226 g
1 oz	30 g
1 teaspoon	5 g

Liquid measure	
1 gallon	4.5 l
1 pint	568 ml
½ pint	284 ml
1 fluid oz	28 ml
1 teaspoon	5 ml

METRIC CONVERSION

Weight		Liquid measures		Temperature	
				Fahrenheit	*Centigrade*
5 lb	2.2 kilos	1 gallon	4.5 litres	70°F	21°C
4 lb	1.8 kilos	½ gallon	2.2 litres	65°F	18°C
3 lb	1.3 kilos	1 pint	568 millilitres	60°F	16°C
2 lb	907 grammes	½ pint	284 millilitres	55°F	13°C
1 lb	453 grammes	1 fluid oz	28 millilitres	50°F	10°C
½ lb	226 grammes	½ fluid oz	15 ml (approx.)	45°F	7°C
¼ lb	113 grammes	¼ fluid oz	8 ml (approx.)	40°F	4°C
1 oz	30 g (approx.)				
½ oz	15 g (approx.)				
¼ oz	8 g (approx.)				

SPECIFIC GRAVITY

Specific gravity	*Weight of sugar*		*Potential alcohol (% by volume)*
	oz per gallon	g per litre	
1.005	3	16	0.3
1.010	5	30	0.6
1.015	7	44	1.4
1.020	9	57	2.2
1.025	11	70	2.9
1.030	13	83	3.7
1.035	15	97	4.5
1.040	17	110	5.2
1.045	19	123	5.9
1.050	21	136	6.7
1.055	23	149	7.4
1.060	26	163	8.2
1.065	28	174	9.0
1.070	30	185	9.7
1.075	32	196	10.5
1.080	34	209	11.2
1.085	36	221	11.9
1.090	38	234	12.7
1.095	40	246	13.5
1.100	43	264	14.2
1.105	45	278	15.0
1.110	47	292	15.8
1.115	49	305	16.5
1.120	51	318	17.3

GLOSSARY

Acetification The oxidation of alcohol to acetic acid caused by a bacterial infection of the wine

Acid The major acids of fruits used in winemaking are malic, citric and tartaric. They are essential to create a healthy fermentation and give interest to the wine

Aerobic, anaerobic Aerobic fermentation takes place in the presence of oxygen and anaerobic fermentation in its absence. Wine yeast cells have the ability to live in both conditions

Airlock A glass or plastic device forming a water trap which prevents the flow of air and airborne micro-organisms into the must while allowing the carbon dioxide produced by the fermentation to escape

Aroma A fragrant, attractive smell derived from the ingredients of fruits and flowers used in making wine. More pronounced in a young wine

Astringency A term used to describe the unpleasant dryness in the mouth which can be caused by excessive amounts of tannin in the wine

Autolysis The breakdown of dead yeast cells by the enzyme systems of the yeast. The decomposition can cause off flavours in the wine if it is left for too long before racking

Bentonite A fining agent consisting of natural clay which has a negative charge and is used to clear hazes caused by proteins which are positively charged

Bloom The velvety sheen found on the skins of grapes and other fruits, composed of wine and 'wild' yeasts, moulds, bacteria and dust

Body A term used to describe the taste and feel of the wine in the mouth. which may be full-bodied, medium or thin

Bouquet The pleasant smell which a mature wine gives off when opened. Young wines convey the perfume of the fruits or flowers, the aroma, but as the wine ages sweet-smelling compounds called esters are formed by the slow oxidation of acids and alcohol

Calyx The outer part of a flower, formed of sepals

Campden tablets Tablets of potassium of sodium metabisulphite used, when dissolved, for sterilising equipment and for adding to musts and wine to suppress spoilage organisms

Cap The fruit pulp which is pushed to the top of the fermenting must by carbon dioxide gas bubbles entrapped between particles of fruit. This cap must be broken up and pushed down frequently to prevent infection and to achieve a good extraction from the fruit

Carbon dioxide The gas given off during the process of fermentation by the conversion of sugar to alcohol. Approximately half the sugar in the must is converted to carbon dioxide and half to alcohol

Character The definite and unmistakable qualities of wine associated with taste, colour and bouquet

Citric acid The main acid of citrus fruits, currants and many soft fruits, e.g. raspberries, loganberries, strawberries and elderberries. It promotes a good fermentation but does little to improve bouquet or flavour

Clarification When fermentation ceases the suspended particles gravitate to the bottom of the container and the wine becomes clear

Colloidal hazes Insoluble cellulose particles can remain in suspension because their electrical charges repel each other. Wines that develop hazes after clearing may be affected by spoilage bacteria

Conservation The safe keeping and protection during the gradual harmonising and maturing period of the wine

Demijohn A glass jar of one gallon capacity used for the fermentation and bulk storage of wine

Dessert wine A sweet, full-bodied wine usually drunk at the end of a meal

Dry wine A wine without any trace of sweetness. Most table wines contain a little residual sugar which is often masked by the degree of acidity but these are generally still classified as dry wines

Effervescence The fizzing seen in a bottle of sparkling wine when it is opened, caused by the release of carbon dioxide bubbles

Enzymes Catalysts produced by living cells which speed up or retard chemical changes. When secreted by wine yeasts their rate of reaction increases at a temperature of 59°F (15°C). They can be destroyed by heat and are inactive in temperatures below 32°F (0°C)

Esters Sweet-smelling compounds formed during maturation of the wine by the slow oxidation of acids and alcohol

Fermentation The breakdown of organic substances by yeast and yeast enzymes. In winemaking this action converts sugars to carbon dioxide and ethyl alcohol. *See also* Pulp fermentation

Glycerol (glycerine) A by-product of fermentation which confers a smoothness to the finished wine

Harsh A wine that is coarse and astringent is described as harsh. This is mainly due to excessive tannin, and such a wine will need longer to mature

Hydrometer An instrument used for measuring the density or thickness of a liquid in which it is floated. In winemaking it is used to measure the amount of sugar present

Infusion The steeping of ingredients in water or wine to extract flavour and colour

Lactic acid A by-product of fermentation in wines, particularly when a malolactic fermentation takes places. The amount of lactic acid is then greatly increased and the malic acid reduced

Lees The sediment that collects at the bottom of the fermentation jar, consisting of dead yeast cells, tartrates and other insoluble salts

Malic acid The principal acid found in apples, cherries, damsons and plums, nectarines, rhubarb, sloes and unripe grapes. It helps in ester-forming reactions, which make a direct contribution to the bouquet of the wine

Malolactic fermentation A fermentation caused by lactobacilli that changes malic acid into lactic acid and carbon dioxide

Maturation The ageing period after fermentation ceases when complex chemical reactions take place. The overall effect will be a reduction in astringency as tannin combines with other components and precipitates out. Time is required to allow for the slow oxidation of acids and alcohol to form esters which bestow bouquet to the wine

Must Fruit juice extract or pulp before fermentation is completed

Oxidation Wine naturally takes up some oxygen from the air which is essential for its development. The quantity required is minimal, however, so careful racking at all times is important to prevent over-oxidation, which causes a brownish tint and impairs the flavour.

Pasteurisation The raising of the temperature of the ingredients to 150°F (66°C) for 5 minutes to enable a quick extraction of flavour and colour and the killing of any bacteria present

Pectin-destroying enzyme A preparation that destroys the pectin in fruits. High levels of pectin may cause a haze in the finished wine

Precipitation As the wines mature the insoluble compounds fall out of solution to form a deposit in the storage vessel

Pulp fermentation Fermentation in the presence of fruit to extract acids, sugars, flavour, tannins, nutrients and vitamins

Residual sugar The sugar remaining in the wine when fermentation ceases

Sediment The accumulation of matter that sinks to the bottom of the fermentation or wine vessel. During fermentation this is often referred to as lees, during maturation as a deposit, and when the wine has cleared as crust or argols

Social wine Wines which may be drunk at any time, without food. These may be medium-dry or medium-sweet, according to taste. The alcoholic content is usually higher than in table wines, ranging from 11 to 14 per cent by volume

Specific gravity The weight of any substance or solution as compared with the weight of an equal volume of water. Water becomes more dense when sugar is added to it and its specific gravity is increased. Alcohol is less dense than water so as the sugar is converted into alcohol the specific gravity is reduced

Stabilising The prevention of refermentation in the presence of residual sugar by racking and the use of sulphite

Stuck fermentation A fermentation that stops prematurely, often caused by excessive amounts of sugar

Sulphite The name most often used when referring to sodium or potassium metabisulphite (Campden tablets), used in solution to sterilise equipment. It is an effective inhibitor of unwanted bacteria and yeast in must and wine

Tannin A substance found in the skins, seeds and stalks of fruits which, due to its astringent qualities, gives character and 'bite' to the wine

Tartaric acid The principal acid found in ripe grapes

Topping-up Each time the wine is racked there is a small loss which leaves air space at the top of the storage vessel. A little water should be added to bring the liquid to within 1 inch of the bung

Vinosity The qualities imparted to the wine by fermentation giving it a 'wine-like' taste and smell

Yeast Single celled micro-organisms, of which there are many species. The one used in winemaking is *Saccharomyces cerevisiae*, variety *ellipsoideus*, which converts the sugars into alcohol

INDEX